# From Refugee to U.S. Soldier

## A Journey of Faith and Success

By: Berhane Amene

# Inspired by, keep moving forward

# DEDICATION:

To my mother, Abrehet Berhe Biru, whose love and sacrifices shaped me; to Jack and Carol Mansfield, whose wisdom, kindness, and unwavering support have been a constant source of strength. To their children, Todd, Jackie, and Scott, whose guidance continues to inspire; to Christie, Todd's loving wife, and all of their children and grandchildren; to Melanie, Scott's devoted wife, and their children and grandchildren; to Pablo, Jackie's husband, and their children, who carry forward the legacy of the Mansfield family.

I also dedicate this to my brothers, sisters, and all of my living relatives and friends, whose support and encouragement have been vital. To the Stark and Shimansky families, and all who have supported me in America—thank you for your kindness.

To the Tigrayans displaced in Sudanese refugee camps—hold on, there is light at the end of the tunnel. Your strength and resilience inspire me. This book is a tribute to the love and determination that bind us all.

## *PREFACE*

*From Refugee to U.S. Soldier: A Journey of Faith and Success* is a gripping memoir of survival, courage, and transformation. At fourteen, I fled war-torn Ethiopia, trekking for days to find freedom in a refugee camp. From there, I embarked on a life-changing journey to Upstate New York, navigating foster care, adapting to a new culture, and discovering purpose in the U.S. military.

Each chapter reveals hard-won lessons of resistance, faith, and hope, showing the power of education and community to overcome life's darkest moments. This is more than a memoir—it's a call to transform adversity into triumph and inspire your journey of faith and success.

My story awaits—step into its pages and lets it ignite your transformation.

# CONTENTS

## CHAPTER OUTLINE

### Chapter 1: **From Refuge to the Classroom**

Fleeing conflict in Ethiopia, the narrator embarks on a journey of survival and hope. Through determination,

Education becomes the key to transforming hardship into opportunity and paving the way for a brighter future.

### Chapter 2: **Building Inner Strength**

Faith and resilience become guiding forces in the uncertainty of foster care. These pillars of strength help the narrator navigate adversity, build character, and prepare for future success.

### Chapter 3: **A Soldier's Journey**

The Military service tests physical and emotional limits, requiring immense sacrifice. Through recovery, personal perseverance, and VA support, the narrator learns to overcome the profound challenges of service.

### Chapter 4: **Redefining Purpose**

Civilian life after the military brings a journey of rediscovery and healing. Reconnecting with family,

9

community, and faith, the narrator redefines their purpose and sets new goals for a fulfilling future.

Chapter 5: **Window to the Past**

Reflecting on America's political divisions and the Tigray conflict in Ethiopia, the narrator explores the lasting impacts of war, displacement, and division. This chapter offers a powerful call for unity and peace in a fractured world.

Chapter 6: **Fresh Start in the South**

A new chapter begins in Florida, where the narrator finds renewal, stability, and belonging. Overcoming challenges, they build a community and embrace resilience and faith as tools for a brighter tomorrow.

## INTRODUCTION: EMBRACING CHANGE

My heart raced as I approached the border, my feet sore and aching after days of marching. I was leaving behind the only place I had ever called home. At only fourteen years old, I had no clear direction, no grand aspirations for the future, just an unwavering determination to survive and seek something better in a cold, unwelcoming world.

Leaving home wasn't a decision; it was a matter of survival. I didn't realize then that this decision would make the beginning of reality more painful than I could have imagined. I would face unexpected obstacles, relying on strong sources I hadn't yet discovered. This moment marked the beginning of a journey that would challenge my resolve and transform my understanding of survival. sept

Amid the uncertainty, I learned that life is shaped not by the conflicts we run from but by the strength we find to move forward. Running away from conflicts may feel like the easiest option, but focusing on persistence, drive, and the overall power within ourselves allows us to overcome the tests and embark on new adventures.

So, my journey began—or rather, continued—in the United States as a young immigrant entering a country with a new language, culture, and way of life. My journey did not end upon reaching the United States; it evolved. The challenges of survival have given way to the complexities of adapting to a new culture and language. Amid the fury of war, displacement, and unyielding chaos, one truth emerged: mere survival was never enough. I yearned for something more profound—learning and fulfilling. Each obstacle I faced became a step, propelling me to a more advanced stage of my journey—from adapting to life as a refugee to navigating the complexities of the American foster care system.

Looking back at the pages of history, September 11, 2001, will always stand out as a day of unparalleled tragedy. People around the World watched in horror as planes struck the towers of the World Trade Center, forever altering the course of history. At the time, I could not fully grasp the magnitude of the misfortune that had befallen the World as the iconic "Twin Towers" collapsed. However, as events unfolded, feelings of grief and a desire for justice took root within me. As the world grappled with the tragedy of September 11, I found myself moved by both grief and a desire for justice. These emotions, shaped by my own experiences of loss and conflict, inspired me to

12

serve in the United States Army. This experience became a defining part of my identity.

Today, I am devoted to serving humanity and working to bring about positive change in a world afflicted by violence, war, and destruction—a world that desperately needs healing and renewal. My time in the military was transformative, installing in me a profound admiration and respect for the power of change and, even more so, for my comrades who shared the journey with me.

Even in my darkest moments, I saw education as a beacon of hope. Later, it became the key to my transformation, empowering me to move from survival to success in fields I once thought unreachable. Education became the pathway to growth and progress, enabling me to realize my vision and use it to assist others. This mindset propelled me to earn advanced degrees in computer science and cybersecurity engineering—fields that once felt entirely unfamiliar. These were not just technical achievements; they represented a pivotal moment, marking a transformative turning point.

This book is not just a narrative or a description of events from my experience but an epilogue that reveals what the human spirit can overcome. It reflects discovering a new version of myself, forged through the battles I endured. My journey began as a young refugee, continued as a soldier in a foreign land, and culminated in achieving my dream of becoming an academic and pursuing justice. Everyone is motivated to grow into a better version of themselves through education and a commitment to serving others.

Sharing my experiences with others offers hope and reshapes perspectives on the challenges people face. No matter how limited or difficult the journey may seem, faith—paired with the unwavering determination to hold things together—becomes a powerful source of strength to overcome the odds. Everyone has the potential to rise beyond the boundaries set by their origins.

This is the story of my struggle-filled journey, one that, in many ways, others may recognize as their own. It captures the essence of a single life, woven with universal threads that connect us all: the longing for belonging, the drive to find purpose, and the profound significance of the journey's return.

My ordeals are unique, as are yours. However, they are part of the broader story of humanity where firm endures, hope prevails, and the will to rise and create a better world for oneself and loved ones defines us all.

But ask yourself, as you explore this story, what lies at the center of your life? In this case, what choice will you make when you arrive at your crossroads? Within these pages is my story of survival and victory, which I pray will resonate with many, empowering them to stand tall and chart their course.

As early as now, I recognize the power of faith. Through every struggle—whether fleeing my country, adapting to an unfamiliar environment, serving in the Army, or facing whatever life threw at me—the hand of God was always there. He was my higher power when everything else was gone; He was the first and last thing I turned to when I had nothing. For those about to begin my story, know that every action I took was motivated by my trust in the Creator and the belief that He had a plan for my life.

## Chapter 1: FROM REFUGEE TO CLASSROOM

There was a prevalent smell of dust and the stifling scent of perspiration, a constant reminder of the looming prospects. The war was audible in the background. Nights were difficult for me, as every slight sound seemed amplified a hundred times in my mind, making my heart race. The refugee camp was more than just a place of geographical displacement; it was a place of both despair and aspiration. Physical fatigue was overwhelming due to the long journey, but the mental exhaustion of merely existing drained my spirit the most. Day after day, the same question haunted me: How long would this last, and would I ever be able to return to my home? Yet, amid that fear and fatigue, there remained a yearning for freedom that would not die. I was not just a passive recipient of events; I was searching for an exit—an opportunity to prove that I could build a better future for myself and my family, regardless of who I was or what I had endured.

### STRUGGLE FOR SURVIVAL

During my fourteenth year, I had to make one of the most complex decisions of my existence. The situation in my homeland, Tigray, Ethiopia, had worsened to the point where staying had become too risky. Our way of life has become increasingly difficult to sustain, disrupted by uncertainty, with daily routines replaced by constant anxiety. The roads, once filled with children playing, people herding their cattle, and simple markets selling local produce, were now harshly quiet, overshadowed by the deafening sound of war drums. Tigray, a region known for its great people and rich cultural heritage, had changed beyond recognition. The place is known as the cradle of civilization; some believe it to be where the arc of convenience resided, and home of the World's major religions, Christians, Muslims, and Jewish communities harmoniously coexist.

First, leaving my home made me feel like I was leaving everything behind: my parents, roots, and reality. However, I had no choice but to run to survive. The decision was about me and not giving up on the dream of a better tomorrow. Even though I was young, I felt the weight of my decision. The gunshots echoing in the air and the survivors' tales of the dead made it clear that there was no reason to stay.

I left home quietly in the dark of the night—the early morning hours—while my parents slept soundly. I chose not to say goodbye or wake them, believing it was better to avoid the emotional scene. As I packed the essentials into my bag, heavy sorrow settled in my chest. The thought that I might never see my family again tore at me. However, the image of calmness outside this chaos kept me moving despite the fear and uncertainty surrounding me.

When others sought shelter and moved to new places, I felt strangely cut off from everything and everyone. We traveled as one unit and didn't share the grief of losing something, but I still felt like I was the only one burdened with more somber thoughts. How could my parents and friends ever forgive me for abandoning them? Would they ever understand the circumstances that led to my decision to leave? Each step I took seemed to bring a new wave of anxiety. I couldn't stop wondering whether my family was safe or if bloodshed had already begun at their home.

It wasn't just a building I was leaving behind but a lifetime of memories and a deep connection to a place. That house held the voices of the people I loved, the joy of laughter once shared, and a comfort that had always been a part of me. I knew that the further I went, the stronger the emotional bond would grow. It felt like the distance between me and every part of that goodbye expanded with each mile.

Would I ever return? I reassured myself that I would, yet something vital remained behind. I had shed my childhood innocence, yet I knew the road ahead would demand an energy I wasn't sure I possessed.

The Tigray region would be considered my home. But for many years, as I grew up, the area was engulfed in violence and conflict that grew into turmoil with little hope of a peaceful resolution. Most of my childhood memories revolve around family values, rich culture, and the strong morals that our people uphold. However, as these ideals began to take shape, they were overshadowed by violence and a relentless sense of helplessness as relatives became enemies and the land turned into a warzone. The communist government continued to conscript young students into the national Army by force, which is every parent's nightmare.

Who was responsible for such violence? At the time, the country was ruled by communist leaders grappling with constant rebellion, the influence of Western ideologies, and

19

ongoing riots and unrest. Freedom fighters wanted to remove the dictatorship and bring the country into a democratic way of governing. As I stand here now, I remember how surely these families' efforts evaporated as tensions grew between parties over ideals whose origins they could no longer remember. Daily living was pleasant without violence—a monotony of happiness. I recall the image of children laughing as they danced in the streets, farmers tirelessly harvesting their fields, families gathering around the dinner table, and people from all over the country streaming into worship ceremonies. I still profoundly cherish the happiness tinged with nostalgia.

As the fighting intensified, ceasefires grew painfully rare. The sounds of celebration were slowly overtaken by the relentless crack of gunfire, replaced by an unsettling silence—not the calm of peace, but a silence heavy with unease and apprehension.

I clearly remember one night when I was about twelve years old: the fighters of the Tigray freedom fighters marched into our small town. They engaged in a fierce shootout with government soldiers. It was very dark, with no lights, and the fearful voices of neighbors gathered inside their homes, which could be heard during the quiet moments. By daylight, everything had changed; some of those whispers were lost in chaos and never heard again.

That night, I learned how precious life is and the circumstances that ultimately forced me to leave for peace of mind. The violence didn't just alter the structure of our community; it reshaped the lives of everyone connected to it in ways we could never have imagined. Among them were our distant relatives who lived next door to us and whose lives perished forever. One of his brothers, now living in Europe, became my close friend.

My departure from my homeland at fourteen was marked by fear as I faced the hurdles of surviving while stepping into the unknown with hope and desperation. The once vibrant community, alive with joy and the rhythms of daily life, was overcome by whispers of fear and an overwhelming sense of dread. The conflict swept in, consuming everything in its path. Friends, neighbors, and children I had grown up with were either dragged away or fled in fear—faces that would be seared into my memory forever. There was hardly any air left to breathe, as it was thick with loss. Every step became heavier, weighed down

21

by the memories of the home I had left behind. The sound of my parents' voices grew more distant with each passing moment.

I can still remember the exact moment I decided to leave. It wasn't just a decision; an act of purity would break from everything that had defined my childhood. My parents didn't know. How could they? I was about to make a choice no child should ever have: to walk away from my family, from the home they had built, from the safety net of their love, and to face the World alone. I had to escape; otherwise, the same fate that had consumed so many others would claim me.

I think of my parents, who used to fold our clothes so neatly, tucking in small, precious items as if they could keep our past safe. Now, left behind, that object represented everything we had built rituals, love, and a life that once belonged to us. It was more than a cherished possession—it was a part of me. Leaving it behind felt like letting go of a piece of my soul.

Leaving Ethiopia was not a choice; it was a necessity. My parents had worked tirelessly to build a life for us based on culture, pride, and family. But as the violence

22

drew nearer, they understood the cost of staying. They spoke of moving to the countryside, but for how long? The remaining meant risking my way. In leaving, I wasn't just fleeing physical danger but the loss of a future. And though my parents remained captive to their love for their homeland, they gave me the power to walk away. It was an unspoken gift, the courage to leave so that I might have a chance at it.

The road ahead was uncertain. I didn't know what lay ahead and couldn't guarantee safety. Yet with only hope, I believed that somewhere beyond the refugee camps and borders, a new hurdle awaited—one where, with all the shattered pieces of my childhood, I could start anew and build something different.

I wasn't just living; I was creating a future, one step at a time. Though I was alone, I was not defeated. I believed I would find my way no matter how far I had to go. In doing so, I carried with me the spirit of my parents and my culture, woven into the very fabric of my being. It was more than just learning a new language and trying to adopt new customs to fit into a new country. It was about redefining myself. Every obstacle I encountered, whether in the classroom or the cafeteria, taught me that belonging is not something you find. You create it through persistence, understanding, and the courage to stand out.

## JOURNEY TO SUDAN

The trip to Sudan was worse than just long and tiring; it was an ordeal that tested every remaining part of me. With every step into that harsh and unforgiving heat, the terrain stripped away another layer of hope, exposing raw survival instincts. The relentless sun made us wretched, our skin scorched, and our lips cracked from thirst. Days without food worried us about our stomachs, each movement a battle against weakness. The shadow of danger was always over us, inescapable, like one we could never outrun. Every noise—be it a distant wind or a snapping twig—felt like a warning. Survival was never a certainty, and we understood that all too well. Pressing on meant taking one step at a time, even when the path ahead felt hopeless.

Revival was never guaranteed, and we knew it; moving forward meant taking one step at a time, even when it felt hopeless. We walked for days without rest, stopping when exhaustion became unbearable. Beneath the fleeting shade of trees or in makeshift shelters, our bodies would collapse in pain. At the same time, our minds wrestled with the torment of an uncertain future. Yet, the physical toll was nothing compared to the emotional weight that pressed down on us.

Fear followed us like a relentless predator, always present, chewing at the edges of our minds. The anxiety of not knowing what lay at the end of this journey was suffocating. With each step, the sorrow of leaving behind all familiar—the land, the people, the spirit that had once been home—grew heavier. The weight of loss felt crushing. Yet, amidst all this darkness, something still endured. A glimmer of hope refused to die. Deep inside me, something continued to push me forward—a determination beyond mere survival. It was this belief—that perhaps across the border, beyond the chaos and violence, there would be safety and a chance to rebuild.

One night, sitting under a tree, the cool night air barely cooling off the heat of the day, my uncle's voice broke the stillness. His words were flat and unwavering, like the earth beneath us. He told stories of our forefathers—those who had endured trials and tribulations beyond our comprehension. "We are their blood," he declared, his voice cutting through the darkness. Resilience is in us. We are not the first to face this and will not be the last. We come from a line of survivors. His stories were more than mere words; they were animation. In that instant, I realized that survival wasn't just about enduring physical hardships but the power of the spirit. It was about carrying on the legacy of those who had come before us—those who faced the impossible and still found a way to survive. Those stories became my armor, my energy source when the journey seemed too much to bear. Survival was no longer just a physical struggle—it became a testimony to the power of the human spirit.

I was walking to escape the danger behind me and head toward the future I would fight to create no matter what the cost. We had been walking all day, and exhaustion clung to us like dust from the road. As we neared the Nile River, hunger began to creep over us; each step felt heavier than the last. Then, seemingly out of nowhere, a man appeared with his cattle. He offered us fresh milk straight from the cow. It felt like the World's weight had been lifted off my shoulders instantly—even if only for a moment. One might think it was a simple act, but it was more than feeding our bodies. To us, it restored a small measure of hope, and that

26

carried us a little farther. But as the days grew longer and the exhaustion more overwhelming, doubt began to set in. One of my fellow travelers, a man who had shared this harrowing journey with me thus far, turned and said he wanted to head back.

The strain had become too great, and he no longer believed we would make it. He slumped to the ground, his face drawn and hollow. He said I can't go any further; this journey will kill us. For a moment, his words sank in—the exhaustion, the hunger, the fear—everything pulling me toward surrender. But something deeper stirred within me. I wasn't ready to give in. "We've come too far," I told him, kneeling beside him. The only way out is to move forward. There's no going back now. We've endured too much to give up when safety could be beyond the horizon. I yanked him up by the arm, my legs barely steady beneath me. We moved forward, though every part of my body screamed for rest. We still had miles to go before reaching the Sudanese border, a city named Kesela. However, the taste of that milk stayed with me, a constant reminder of the kindness and humanity one can find even in the bleakest of times.

It was then that I realized that our survival would not come from sheer energy alone but from the strength we found in supporting one another. Together, we would press on—not as individuals but as a unified force, bound by our shared determination to move forward.

The temporary refugee camp became my new reality. The air was thick with the smell of dust and sweat, a constant reminder that the energy I had known had crumbled.

And at night, the distant sounds of battle pierced the stillness, sending shivers down my spine. Sleep was no longer a refuge; fear had replaced it. The camp was not just a place where we were displaced physically but also a battleground where hope and despair wrestled for dominance. My body ached from the journey, but survival weighed even heavier on my mind. Every day brought the same painful question: When will this end? Will I ever go home?

But deep inside, something refused to die sure fire. I wasn't just a victim of the circumstances that forced me to flee; I was a fighter. I wasn't going to let the conflict define me. Amid all the fear and loss, one thing remained with me:

education. It became my lifeline, my anchor in a sea of uncertainty. I told myself that if I could learn, I would be OK to shape my future, not defined by the war that tore my soul apart. The day I left, I carried a little beyond a few belongings and the World's weight on my shoulders. But I also brought the memories of my friends and family, who had given so much to make us a home. I leave because we have no choice; we run because the flames behind us give us no time to mourn what we've lost.

The two years I spent in Sudan were the longest of my time. Each day was a struggle for survival, filled with unexpected setbacks. I spent most of my time in small, grayish rooms without air conditioning, fighting the stifling humidity that made the nights unbearably hot. Many of us resorted to sleeping outside in search of a breeze. My thoughts were engulfed by the desire to return to the border, join the freedom fighters, or find another way to move forward. My soul felt suspended—neither here nor there. A glimmer of optimism appeared when we registered with the United Nations High Commissioner for Refugees. They began assisting us, offering a chance to break free from this endless cycle and seek a better future in a developed country. Even then, resettlement seemed like an improbable dream out of reach. The process of registering and getting better at it was not easy, but eventually, we succeeded in our vision.

Since one of our family members was already in Sudan, logistics and getting around the city became routine. We helped navigate the complexities of the immigration system. In the late 1980s, thousands of Ethiopian Jews fled to Sudan and were on the pipeline to migrate to Israel. Among them were friends of mine who, as refugees, wanted nothing more than to reach Israel. They patiently awaited airlift to Israel in what became later famously known as "Operation Solomon" (Mivtza Shalomo). A year after we arrived in the United States, we received the news that thousands of Ethiopian Jews had already been transported to Israel under this historic operation.

Meanwhile, many non-Jewish Ethiopians, including us, were in the immigration pipeline, awaiting an opportunity to resettle in a new land. Though we received an invitation to register by a third party to immigrate to Israel, moving to America was our dream. The choice we made was deeply rooted in our Christian faith. America became the destination of choice, a land whose values and ideals

30

seemed to align with ours. After years of uncertainty, the day we were chosen for resettlement to the United States felt surreal, like a long-awaited dream finally coming true. The year 1990 changed our lives forever. I had spent so much time focusing on day-to-day survival that living felt foreign. My two years in Sudan taught me not to expect anything and to take each day as it came. But as the plane touched down in New York, the reality of what lay ahead hit me, and there, the Statue of Liberty shone brightly. The problem I was leaving behind was caused by another one I didn't quite understand.

Stepping off the plane in Binghamton, Upstate New York, I entered a world unfamiliar. The streets were lined with well-kept houses, and the air was crisp and cool. Binghamton was a quiet, green city that blended suburban charm with natural beauty: well-manicured lawns, wide streets, and peaceful neighborhoods seemed straight out of a storybook. At the time, however, the rapid pace of being felt alien to me. I soon realized that my struggle for survival had not ended; it had simply taken a different form.

The anxiety of beginning a new chapter was matched only by the profound relief of arriving in a country that promised safety and opportunity. It was the start of forging a new life against all odds. Yet, the uncertainties of this foreign land quickly replaced the familiar uncertainty that had shaped my spirit in Sudan. Yet, for the first time, the hope that the UN-US refugee settlement programs have instilled in our hearts began to feel real. Of course, the most immediate and daunting setback I faced was not knowing the language. More important than any foreign language, English was to become the key to my future. Without it, I felt isolated, unable to express my basic thoughts. Every interaction, from school to the grocery store, became a hurdle. Words that fell from everyone else's mouth so easily stuck in my throat, constantly reminding me of how I was an outsider in a world where getting communication right was a matter of existence.

Another new experience awaited me at the dinner table: American food tasted different, yet I was eager to try something new. Before long, pizza and burgers became staples, a small part of American culture I learned to enjoy. I kept myself busy with sports, watching the news, reading anything I saw on my way, and trying to make sense of it.

32

Learning English as a second language continued for a long time to come.

My first days at school were a confusing mixture of excitement and fear. Everything felt foreign—from the language to how people dressed, pieces of a puzzle I wasn't sure I could solve. The class buzzed with energy, and I struggled to understand even a few words amidst the easy chatter and laughter of the students. It was like I'd been dropped into a film where everyone knew their lines, but I'd forgotten mine. She introduced me to the class, and my name sounded awkward and foreign as it rolled off her tongue. I smiled, though anxiety had taken over my stomach. The names of the other students in my class sounded unfamiliar, strange, and challenging to remember. Every time they introduced themselves, the words slipped away before I could grasp them, making me feel more and more like an outsider with each passing moment.

Even though I occasionally sat with classmates at lunchtime, I sometimes chose solitude to observe my surroundings better until my known friends arrived. Meanwhile, sitting at the cafeteria to eat, staring at food that was utterly foreign to me, became the norm. The smells, textures, and even the way people ate were unfamiliar. It felt like the dining hall teased my tray; I didn't know how to fit in or what to say if someone approached me. In those moments, I felt lonelier than before. My experience felt so personal that very few others could understand. I often thought that nobody in that entire school had gone through or was experiencing anything like what I was feeling. It was as though I were invisible in my uniqueness, carrying the heavy burden of displacement and the struggle of navigating a new language and culture. Despite these obstacles, I knew I had no choice but to adapt—failure was not an option. The students who attended the school were excellent; almost everyone was friendly and very nice to me. Those who do not know me have no idea that I am from another continent. We didn't have electronics to distract us from the social interactions essential to our daily lives; no phones kept us glued to screens.

In contrast, integrating electronics into today's education offers a unique and irreplaceable advantage, reshaping how students learn and connect. The value of perseverance, resilience, and the unwavering belief that education was and still is the key to overcoming adversity. These lessons

34

fueled my determination to learn English, no matter how difficult it seemed.

When I became an American thirty years ago, I desired to hold onto the values of my Tigray-Ethiopia heritage. However, I also needed to adapt to my new home. At times, it felt like balancing on a tightrope between two worlds: one demanding adaptation and change, the other reminding me of who I was and where I came from.

The cultural differences between where I came from, and the U.S. were large. In Tigray, community and family were the heart of everything. Our lives were deeply connected with the group's well-being, often prioritizing individual needs. Customs and faith were seamlessly woven into the fabric of our daily existence, shaping our values and guiding our actions. In America, I encountered a different pattern. There was more emphasis on individualism, personal success, and independence, efficiency, progress, and self-reliance were highly valued— principles I respected but at times which were complex for me to reconcile with my own

Sometimes, this cultural dissonance weighed heavily on me. There were moments when I thought this could be a place where I might fit in, as the surroundings contrasted sharply with the environment where I had grown up. However, as I learned to navigate the expectations of my new home, I found ways to adapt without losing sight of the values that had shaped me: a sense of community, faith, and resilience that had carried me through conflict, which continued to guide me in this new chapter.

I embraced certain aspects of American culture, such as its openness, opportunities, and belief in the power of education. Yet, I held fast to the values instilled in me by my parents and country: a sense of responsibility toward family, the importance of humility, and a deep respect for the community.

Though tested by my new environment, these values remained intact and shaped how I approached every obstacle. However, as I stood at the threshold of a new phase, the future was uncertain. Would this value set be enough to see me through the trials ahead? While I had survived the journey into a new land, I now faced a new kind of battle—one in which survival required more than the will to endure. It would mean adapting, evolving, and holding on to the very core of myself while navigating a mysterious world.

Would the sacrifices I made be worth it? Could I succeed in this foreign land while remaining true to my roots? As I contemplated the future, I couldn't help but ask myself: how much of myself would I have to leave behind to move forward?

I knew the answers wouldn't come quickly. The road ahead was both promising and uncertain. But one thing was clear: my journey was far from over, and my trials were beginning. As I pressed on, I carried with me the weight of my past and the hope that the future would reveal who I could become and how far I could go. Though I had no map or plan, there was one truth I retained: God was guiding my steps. Any flashes of fear and doubt vanished with one silent thought: I was never alone. It was foundational faith that propelled me forward when my power faltered.

## FROM REFUGEE TO CLASSROOM

Susquehanna Valley High School, NY - 1994 Yearbook:
A lasting collection of unforgettable moments and
milestones from a year that forever shaped my journey.

1993 SV High School the Soccer Team

## Chapter 2: BUILDING INNER STRENGTH

At the very moment I entered my first foster home, the feeling of *displacement* weighed heavily on my body. This change felt different from all the others I had faced. New faces, beds, and a new way of living, as if it belonged to someone else, never allowed me to catch my breath. A faint smell of cleaning supplies lingered in the air, and the house's quiet seemed to carve loneliness into my soul. To me, foster care is more than just a system—it represents the art of survival.

Foster care in the United States serves as a safety net for children who, due to unsafe or unstable conditions, cannot remain with their biological families. While foster care offers protection, it also presents significant emotional and psychological ordeals. These hurdles are especially common for children, who must navigate the system's complex and often transient nature. For many, living becomes a series of disruptions. Without consistent relationships or a stable home environment, feelings of isolation, uncertainty, and abandonment are common. In such circumstances, losing track of one's identity and sense of belonging is easy.

No child entering foster care has the same experience. Some are placed in long-term homes receiving care and love, while others move from one house to another, struggling to form lasting connections. Every new placement introduces different rules, dynamics, and emotional adjustments. Many described such an energy of constant movement as exhausting, leaving them emotionally drained and with little direction for the future. I, too, felt this dislocation, but my journey was different. I entered the system at an older age, giving me a certain emotional maturity level that other children lacked.

While many foster care kids tried to understand the world, I focused on surviving and learning. This emotional maturity fostered resilience, helping me navigate the system while maintaining a degree of emotional distance from it. Often, I found myself in the role of quiet protector, especially for the younger children who struggled with the confusion and trauma that usually accompany foster care. In this restrained space, where their dislocation still lingered, I understood early on while supporting others. I also needed to find my path to healing.

Foster care redefined my understanding of robustness. It wasn't about suppressing emotions or facing trials alone; actual energy lay in adaptability, finding ways to thrive amid uncertainty, and seeking community support to navigate complexities. I was mature and consistently followed the rules, a quality that earned the approval of my foster parents. One of the values I demonstrated was a commitment to continuous learning, often spending hours reading, which reflected my determination to grow. Additionally, I helped my foster parents in any way I could, further earning their trust and admiration. They often expressed pride in my behavior, sometimes even wishing the other children would adopt the values I embodied.

Education became my refuge, the place where I could regain control and work toward a future independent of the notions of foster care instability. The scent of freshly sharpened pencils and the quiet rustling of paper during class kept me grounded when everything else seemed to fall apart. Every assignment completed and every test passed became a testament to my ability to succeed against

43

all odds. Education wasn't just a way forward; it became the guidance I retained in an unpredictable world out of my control.

While education shaped my intellectual energy, spiritual growth fortified my emotional resilience. Every Sunday, I pursued comfort in church—attending an Assembly of God congregation, then a Catholic church, and later a Presbyterian one. The church became more than a place of worship; it was a refuge, a sanctuary filled with warmth and music that allowed me to forget the uncertainties of foster care momentarily. The smell of varnished wood and wax from candles greeted me as I entered, while the murmur of voices praying wrapped around me like a hug. Volunteering while the soft murmur of prayers enveloped me like a warm embrace, volunteers greeted us with open arms. The soft rustling of hymnals passed around filled the air, and at that moment, the weight I carried seemed to ease, if only briefly.

I found acceptance and spiritual leadership in the church. The musical worship services, filled with a shared sense of unity, helped me understand what was happening to me. I recall the deep resonance of the organ and the voices of everyone singing together, which seemed to lift the weight from my chest. During these sermons, the teachings began to shape my understanding of resilience.

Over time, I saw energy not as a solitary burden on the shoulder but as a strength nurtured through faith and community. The kindness of the church members extended beyond the church walls, spilling into activities they organized, such as lunches, camping trips, and other community functions. These events provided a steady source of joy and continuity amidst the uncertainty of foster care. These moments of fellowship revealed that spiritual strength arises through connection with others and a higher power.

Looking back, I see my spiritual growth intertwined with my experiences in the system. In both, I learned invaluable lessons in resilience, patience, and the power of community.

The church became a space to reflect on tribulations while ideas of a hopeful and possible future took shape. It provided a conceptual framework that connected my place in the world with the belief that my journey had a purpose.

My first foster family in Conklin, New York, played a significant role. I lived with that kind of family for over a year while attending Susquehanna Valley High School. Living in their home provided stability, allowing me to nurture my education while immersing myself in American culture. The house always carried the faint smell of baked bread, which made me feel like something warm was waiting for me. After years of chaos, the quiet hum of family living was comforting. This family provided the structure I needed during that critical juncture, offering me the security to grow and adapt. There was everything teenage children needed: basketball court, swimming, camping, and all other leisure activities.

This family fostered several children at any given time during my stay with them—usually three or four. We all attended school, though the length of our stays varied. Some children would come and go almost instantly, while others, notably boys, stayed longer. Through it all, the family was committed to ensuring each child's success in a stable and supportive environment. They instilled in me, both through words and example, the values of hard work and discipline in persevering through tasks. They modeled resilience, and I internalized these lessons, applying them

46

daily to my studies. Leaving them was bittersweet, but I left on good terms, deeply grateful for their foundational support.

After living with one family for over a year, I moved to another house during the summer. What initially proved to be a disconcerting experience ultimately contributed to my growth. Each foster family brought its own dynamics, traditions, and daily routines, and every new environment required me to approach belonging differently. Through these transitions, I learned that belonging doesn't always equate to fitting in; it requires hard work from the family and finding one's niche within that unique structure.

Transitions weren't always easy but shaped my understanding of adaptability and flexibility. Each experience reinforced the core lesson that strength isn't about never feeling lost or afraid; it's about pushing forward despite those feelings. It's about finding ways to thrive, even when the future seems uncertain and daunting. Over time, I learned that most of the fears I envisioned never materialized.

## FINDING A GUIDING LIGHT

After moving through the uncertainty of two different foster homes, I finally found a place I could call home with my third foster family. That remarkable couple gave me more than just the basics; they gave me a sense of belonging that went far beyond shelter and sustenance. I wasn't just another child they took in; I was part of the family.

A high school teacher was the first angel in the house to notice me in her classroom. Beneath my quiet exterior, she recognized my passion for learning. She understood my obstacles and took a keen interest in my journey. One day, after class, she invited me to her home. Little did I know that this invitation would change my future. My initial question concerned the whereabouts of the books—I had always assumed that every teacher's home would be brimming with textbooks.

Their spacious home, inhabited by just two people, stood atop a hill overlooking the city. When I entered the door, I was greeted by the comforting aroma of freshly brewed coffee and homemade chocolate cookies, mingling with the warmth conveyed by the framed family photos on

48

the walls. It was a place that felt instantly welcoming—not a mere stop along the way, but a sanctuary where roots could finally take hold. Over time, they became more than just guardians; they grew into mentors, advocates, and, most importantly, my family.

One vivid memory that stands out was the time I suffered a severe injury to my ankle, breaking the bone. I rushed to the hospital, where a four-hour surgery was performed to insert a metal screw into my ankle. Recovery demanded a year on crutches, but the injury healed fully. My ankle became more potent than ever, enduring even the rigorous physical demands of my later service in the Army. What left the most lasting impression, however, was the extraordinary generosity of those who covered the cost of the operation—a kindness for which I remain profoundly grateful.

Their belief in me instilled the confidence I needed to believe in myself. They showed me that family isn't just about blood; it's about the love, support, and guidance we offer one another. Through them, I learned that actual energy lies within a community: the people who stand by you in uncertain times, offering the unyielding belief that

49

hope can exist even in the most challenging situations. To this day, they remain a source of energy and inspiration.

They taught me that courage is not merely about enduring hardship; it's about thriving, evolving, and giving back. In hindsight, the resilience I developed from foster care, faith, and the support of those around me has become a cornerstone of who I am today. This resilient person deeply understands the meanings of perseverance, hope, and belonging.

Looking back, I see a journey that continually brought me to one persistent question: Was my courage enough to face the unknown challenges ahead? The security I found in foster care, faith, and community gave me a sense of belonging, a fragile reprieve from the chaos of the past. Yet, the vastness and uncertainty of the world beyond these safe spaces loomed over me. Though my resolve was tested repeatedly, I knew the battle for survival was far from over. Each challenge had forged my determination, but more significant trials awaited. Survival would demand unwavering resilience, steadfast hope, and the strength to press forward, no matter the odds.

Would this built-up resilience be enough to withstand the storms ahead, or would the weight of my past threaten to shatter under the pressure of new trials? Often, in quiet moments of reflection, I wondered if the stability I had cultivated within myself would suit the passage through.

It was a future filled with both opportunity and adversity. I had learned to rise repeatedly, yet I knew that would bring more difficulties to test my endurance and the core of my will. The task was complete, yet its enduring strength remained uncertain—a mystery that only the passage of time could unravel.

Whenever I faced lack and hunger, I turned to God for guidance. Uncertain of what lay ahead, I held onto hope, trusting that His plan would lead to something good. Each day, I prayed, believing that He would guide me through this period of waiting and uncertainty.

## CHOOSING FAITH OVER FEAR

In my journey, I've understood that fear often grips us most tightly in our vulnerable areas: health, finances, and relationships. What do people fear the most? Commonly, it's illness, aging, financial insecurity, or the judgment of others. Yet faith offers transparency. By surrendering these worries to God, we create the space to step back, gain perspective, and recognize that fear amplifies our problems beyond their proportions. This perspective shift allows us to focus on what truly matters and release what disturbs our peace.

The real struggle lies in consistently adopting this approach. As athletes train to harden their bodies, we must train our minds to recognize and dismiss fear-driven, negative thoughts. Faith is the practice that builds resilience, allowing us to replace worry with confidence. However, it needs to be put into action daily for long-term use.

This perspective empowers us to focus on what benefits us while letting go of what holds us back. By identifying and releasing fearful thoughts, we empower our mental resilience. Faith and hope are connected, shaping how we view the world and approach its trials, believing without seeing. Faith provides a sense of grounding, equipping us to face life uncertainties confidently. As we nurture a resilient mindset, fear fades into a simple whisper, no longer a controlling force. Embracing faith inspires

52

motivation, instills the courage to overcome obstacles, and fosters the wisdom to value what matters.

At its core, fear is an inevitable part of it, but it doesn't have to define us. Through faith, we gain the energy to overcome what once seemed overwhelming. Faith invites us to embrace it with hope, pursuing the future with clarity and resilience.

## LIVING WITH PURPOSE

Living a life of purpose is more than just achieving goals or fulfilling external expectations; it's about aligning your daily actions with your deepest beliefs and values. When you live intentionally, each decision becomes an opportunity to affirm who you are and what you stand for. This process requires self-awareness and reflection, as it involves identifying what matters most to you and making conscious choices that reflect those priorities.

At the core of intentional living is the concept of *personal values*, the principles that guide our behavior and decisions. These values might include integrity, compassion, family, service, or resilience. They form the bedrock upon which we build our actions, relationships, and career paths. The more closely we align our actions with these values, the more meaningful and fulfilling our lives become.

For example, when you prioritize *honesty and integrity* in every aspect of your life, your actions reflect those values. You might be transparent in your relationships, act ethically in your professional life, and stand up for what's right, even when it's complicated. Living authentically and consistently with your values creates a sense of alignment

54

that provides peace of mind, strengthens your relationships, and allows you to face challenges with confidence and clarity.

Living with purpose also involves being proactive rather than reactive. It means setting goals that aim for success in conventional terms and honoring your core values. It could mean pursuing a career that allows you to help others, dedicating time to volunteer work that aligns with your principles or spending quality time with loved ones who share similar values. Life feels more purposeful when your actions are in harmony with your values, and even the mundane tasks become significant.

Another important aspect of living with purpose is resilience. Aligning your actions with your values often requires perseverance, especially when external pressures or life challenges test your resolve. In these moments, clearly understanding your core values provides a steady foundation. You can draw strength from knowing that you are living by what you truly believe, which helps you navigate adversity with grace and determination.

Moreover, *living with purpose* doesn't mean having a perfect life. It's about striving to grow, learn, and evolve while connecting deeply to your principles. It means making choices that reflect who you want to become rather than who others expect you to be. By embracing this mindset, you create a life that is uniquely yours—one that's authentic, rich in meaning, and aligned with your heart's deepest desires.

In the end, living with purpose allows you to find true fulfillment. It empowers you to live a life that is not only successful by traditional standards but also deeply connected to the things that matter most, giving you a sense of satisfaction beyond fleeting achievements and providing you with a sense of peace and contentment that lasts a lifetime.

These photos capture moments from my high school years and my time in uniformed service.

1996 After High School Graduation

2007 Dedication and Farewell Award

Washington DC Veteran Memorial

2003 Fort Knox Soldier's Basic Training

## Chapter 3: SOLDIER'S JOURNEY

Weeks before Iraq's dictator, Saddam Hussein, was captured, I found myself facing one of the most challenging experiences of my life: The United States Army basic training at Fort Knox, Kentucky. It was January 2003, and the cold bit through every layer of clothing like a relentless adversary. While the world's focus remained fixed on the chaos unfolding in Iraq, my battle was far more personal and closer to home. Each day was a grueling test of physical endurance, mental grit, and emotional fortitude. I hadn't fully anticipated but one that would shape me in ways I never imagined.

The training schedule began before dawn, jolting us awake with the drill sergeant's booming commands. His voice was our unwelcome alarm, summoning us to the field where the day's trials awaited. From the moment we stepped outside, the hours ahead were grueling— unforgiving physical provocation, relentless tactical drills, and exercises designed to push our mental endurance to the brink. Every task was deliberate, engineered to shatter our perceived limits and rebuild us as soldiers.

Fort Knox wasn't just a training ground but a crucible—a place that tested us in ways we couldn't have imagined. Known for its all-male Army programs, it stripped away every facade, forcing us to confront our most profound weaknesses and fears. The process was brutal but purposeful. It wasn't just about preparing us for the physical demands of war—it was about readying us for the battles within ourselves. Long before we set foot on foreign soil, the war had already begun in our minds.

The obstacle courses, endless marches in full gear through bone-chilling cold, and relentless drills filled every waking moment. Each test dragged us to the edges of endurance. Yet, those moments of pain revealed something deeper: resilience, discipline, and unity. These weren't just buzzwords; they became our foundation, the unshakable core of who we were becoming. Training wasn't just about mastering weapons or maneuvers but mastering ourselves. It taught us to press forward when every part of us screamed to stop.

Misery and Agony Hills became enduring symbols of our shared struggle as silent witnesses to the pain, perseverance, and determination that defined those grueling days. They left a lasting impact on us—not just as soldiers, but as individuals. That training forged more than skills; it forged character. Nearly half of the trainees couldn't overcome those hills and had to restart their training. I was fortunate to succeed. Growing up in one of the most rugged terrains in the world gave me a unique advantage, preparing me for obstacles that others found insurmountable. Joining the Army with a college degree gave me a higher rank and pay scale than many fellow soldiers. My education was pivotal throughout, influencing my opportunities and enhancing my ability to contribute effectively.

During this intense period, one thing kept me grounded—a quiet, unwavering source of pride: earning my bachelor's degree. To many, a college degree might seem like just a piece of paper. However, it symbolizes a decade of hard work, sacrifice, and perseverance. It stood for countless late nights of studying, balancing multiple jobs, and confronting the hurdles life threw at me as an immigrant. That diploma wasn't just an academic milestone—it was my badge of honor. It reminded me that no obstacle could keep me from reaching my goals, no matter how daunting.

There are many reasons why I remained committed to staying in school, but one stands out vividly. I remember my parents selling their precious belongings during my first grade to cover my school expenses. They valued education above all else, believing it was more important than any material possession we could ever acquire.

I realized how unique my journey had been when training alongside fellow recruits at Fort Knox. Many of my peers had followed different paths to get here. However, my road—from a refugee camp to the lecture halls of an American university—was never far from my thoughts. That journey, shaped by struggle and resilience, had unknowingly prepared me for the rigors of training. My degree wasn't just an accomplishment, a lifeline, or a source of motivation. It reminded me of the hope my family and I had attached to and the future we had worked so hard to build.

I leaned on that hope as the training days grew longer and more grueling. Exhaustion tested my limits, but I drew energy from remembering all I had overcome. I knew I had to be prepared to face whatever challenges arose, whether on the battlefield or beyond. Fort Knox was shaping me into a soldier. However, long before I wore the uniform, I

64

learned the values of perseverance and determination. The discipline I hoped to pursue in my education now guided me through this new chapter. I didn't know the future but knew I was ready to face it head-on.

## GRATITUDE THROUGH SERVICE

Enlisting in the Army was not a spur-of-the-moment decision; it resulted from years of reflection and a deep gratitude for the country that offered me a second chance. I left behind a life marked by conflict, uncertainty, and hardship, seeking refuge from instability and violence. When I arrived in the United States, I found safety and the promise of a future I had never imagined. This country opened doors to opportunities I once thought was beyond reach, instilling a profound sense of duty to give back. The kindness and security I received became a constant source of motivation, and sacrifice seemed the most direct and honorable way to repay that debt.

While a sense of duty drove my decision to enlist, it was also deeply personal. I often reflected on my parents' sacrifices to create a better life for me, leaving their culture, community, and homeland behind. Their courage in the face of the unknown and their resilience in enduring hardship shaped the core of my values. Every struggle they faced was worthwhile if it meant I could access the education, stability, and opportunities they had dreamed of for me. Their perseverance laid the foundation for my commitment to serve.

Standing on the training grounds at Fort Knox, preparing to serve the country that had embraced me, I felt an overwhelming sense of purpose. It was about pursuing my ambitions and honoring the journey that had led me to this moment. I carried the weight of the sacrifices that had made my path possible and deeply understood the significance of the opportunity granted. I knew I had to make it count—not just for myself but for every refugee, immigrant, and individual who left behind a familiar life in search of a new beginning. At Fort Knox, I realized the enormity of that responsibility. I was not just preparing to serve but honoring the past and contributing to a future filled with possibility.

Values like duty and loyalty were instilled in me long before I wore a uniform. These principles were deeply rooted in my upbringing and reinforced by the military traditions of my third foster family. The husband in that family, a former Marine officer, embodied a quiet, strong, and unwavering dedication that left a lasting impression on me. Their household represented the discipline, resilience, and purpose I aspired to live by, making my decision to enlist a natural extension of my values. It allowed me to contribute to something larger than myself, grounded in personal and shared ideals.

For me, joining the Army was more than just a career move; it was a calling. By enlisting, I honored the legacy of resilience and perseverance modeled throughout my life. My parents' strength, forged through their struggles, fueled me through the demanding days of basic training. Every push-up, every march, every test of endurance reminded me of the threats they had faced and the power I had inherited. Their determination to overcome adversity mirrored my own, instilling the resolve to continue.

But my decision to enlist was not just about honoring resilience but contributing to something greater than myself. By joining the Army, I committed to the ideals that had given me a new life: freedom, opportunity, and justice. These principles had transformed my life, providing a fresh start, and I felt responsible for protecting them. I wanted to ensure that others like me could continue to find refuge and hope in the United States. This country had become my

67

sanctuary, and I was determined to preserve it for future generations.

In the military, I found more than just a place to serve— I found a community of individuals who shared the same sense of purpose. We came from diverse backgrounds, each carrying our own stories, yet united by a commitment to protect the nation that had given us so much. This bond transcended camaraderie: it became a personal affirmation of my gratitude and loyalty to the country that had welcomed me. This unity, shared with others who understood its weight, further solidified my sense of belonging and purpose.

Through my duty, I aimed to demonstrate that my inherited toughness and resilience could live on through me. As I persevered through my hardships, I was determined to rise to meet the trials ahead. More than that, I wanted to contribute to something lasting—to leave a legacy of service to the American people that honored the journey that brought me here and ensured the opportunities I had fought to secure would remain available to others for generations. My duty was not simply a chapter of my life but a commitment to a larger vision of a world where hope, freedom, and opportunity are accessible to all who seek a better life.

There were moments when I questioned whether I could make it through. When the weight of my gear felt unbearable or fatigue clouded my focus, I had to dig deep to find the strength to continue. But in those moments of doubt, I discovered the most profound truths about myself. Basic training wasn't just about molding soldiers—it was about transforming individuals into those capable of enduring, adapting, and overcoming. The lessons I learned during that time have remained a constant reminder that no challenge is unbeatable when you possess the will to continue.

Looking back on my weeks at Fort Knox, I recognize that those moments were some of the most formative of my life. Basic training went beyond building physical endurance; it was a journey toward developing mental toughness and resilience, uncovering inner durability I hadn't realized existed. The relentless challenges pushed me to my limits, fostering a deeper understanding of discipline, unity, and purpose. This period marked significant personal growth, where lessons in internal fortitude proved just as valuable as any tactical skills I gained.

Joining the Army was one of the most significant decisions of my life. It wasn't just the start of a career—it was a commitment to something far more critical than mine. It was a way to honor my family's legacy, give back to the country that provided me with a new life, and prove that I could conquer any difficulty. Basic training laid the groundwork for everything that followed.

The core values I embraced during those early weeks—perseverance, strength, and the power of community—continue to resonate with me today. They shape my approach to each new challenge, reminding me that no obstacle is impossible with the right mindset and a solid support system. Looking back, I see that it wasn't just a chapter in my life; it was a defining experience that has shaped the person I am today.

But beyond personal obstacles, basic training instilled a profound appreciation for unity. We quickly learned that no matter how strong or capable we were as individuals, our effectiveness depended on the group's collective strength. Success is immeasurable by personal glory but by the team's unity. This lesson became clear through team-based exercises that demanded flawless coordination. One person's misstep affected the entire group, highlighting the critical importance of shared effort.

We learned to watch out for each other, to provide support when needed, and to celebrate our victories as a unified team. Together, we built resilience and strength that no individual effort could achieve. The bond we formed during those weeks became unbreakable, forged in the crucible of shared hardship and a common purpose.

Each challenge we faced was not just a test of physical stamina but an opportunity for personal growth—to uncover reserves of strength we didn't know we had. It became clear that basic training wasn't solely about preparing for the physical demands of military life. It was about evolving into individuals who could confront adversity with courage and determination. In overcoming the trials of basic training, I realized that the struggle of military life was not just about mastering physical endurance. It was about cultivating the inner resilience needed to navigate whatever lay ahead.

One of the most powerful lessons I took from basic training was the actual value of camaraderie. The military system thrives on the relationships between soldiers, and the bonds we formed during training were not just

71

coincidental. They forged through shared experiences, collective tests, and the realization that our success relied on one another. We hailed from diverse backgrounds, each with our own stories. However, those differences melted away in the trenches of basic training. What remained was the understanding that we were all in this together. The men and women I trained with became more than fellow recruits—they became my brothers and sisters in arms.

Together, we faced exhaustion, frustration, and moments of doubt that pushed us beyond what we thought we could endure. Whether running long distances in formation, navigating obstacle courses, or responding to the unyielding commands of our drill sergeants, we leaned on one another for support. We shared not only physical burdens but emotional ones as well. When someone struggled—whether it was keeping pace or pushing through a particularly challenging driller lifted each other. In those moments, I realized the true essence of brotherhood: it wasn't just about standing side by side; it was about carrying one another when we couldn't stand alone.

The Army taught me early on that no soldier stands alone. This lesson extended beyond the immediate challenges of basic training; it spoke to the deeper purpose of wearing the uniform. We learned to trust one another in our lives, knowing that this trust would be critical. Our bonds tested daily—whether during weapons drills or tactical maneuvers. There was no room for doubt or selfishness. Our collective survival depended on the strength of our relationships and our ability to function as a cohesive unit. In civilian life, friendships often evolve slowly through shared interests; however, camaraderie in the military was forged through shared struggles and sacrifices.

The friendships we formed during those grueling weeks became our lifelines. Sometimes, all it took was a word of encouragement during a long march or a shared laugh after a tough day to keep us going. We didn't need grand gestures to show support for one another. A simple act—like sharing a canteen of water during a break or nudging someone who was faltering—reinforced the belief that we were stronger together than we could ever be alone.

Basic training is designed to test each of us individually, but the real test was how well we could function as a team. Regardless of how fit or mentally tough we were on our own, success relied on our collective effort. The sense of unity that developed during those weeks was profound. It shifted the focus from personal ambition to team toughness. Each of us was responsible for the other, creating an unbreakable bond. In the most challenging moments— when exhaustion set in and the obstacles seemed overwhelming, it wasn't the fear of personal failure that fueled my determination, but the fear of letting down my fellow recruits. That sense of duty pushed us to give more than we thought we could.

Even when our bodies ached, and our minds felt worn down, we found the strength to keep moving forward, knowing our comrades were doing the same.

After completing basic training, I received my assignment to Germany, marking the beginning of a new phase in my military career. The grueling pace of basic training gave way to a different challenge, no longer solely focused on overcoming immediate physical tests. Instead, it became about mastering discipline and routines, where each task carried profound significance. In Germany, our focus shifted from personal endurance to operational readiness, with a constant awareness that we were preparing for real-world scenarios. Every drill and exercise was not mere practice but preparation for deployment into a conflict zone.

This phase of my career heightened my awareness of the immense responsibilities we carried. We were no longer recruits; we were soldiers entrusted with the readiness to serve immediately. The environment in Germany marked this shift—days spent in mission preparation and drills. Yet, beneath it all, there was a constant undercurrent of anticipation, a quiet awareness that some of our skills tested in combat.

The pressure was different from basic training but just as intense, carrying a weight that lingered with every passing moment. Our training was no longer just about physical endurance; we were also learning to adapt mentally and emotionally to challenges that could arise at any moment. Adaptability became the cornerstone of our training, teaching us to remain composed and focused even in the face of uncertainty.

Daily life in Germany became familiar, but it was far from ordinary. Early mornings, rigorous drills, and an unyielding sense of duty shaped me in ways I had not anticipated. Each day presented new challenges, instilling a profound sense of purpose. The armed forces became an intrinsic part of who I was, fostering a deep commitment to my fellow soldiers, my country, and our shared mission.

The camaraderie built during basic training only grew stronger as we faced the demands of this new chapter together. We weren't just training for training's sake—we were preparing for potential deployment, where our skills could mean the difference between success and failure.

Living and working in Germany allowed me to transition from military to civilian life more fully. The structure and discipline reinforced values I had always held—resilience, adaptability, and a deep sense of purpose. Each day reminded me that my role as a soldier involved more than just myself; it was part of something greater. I was part of an organization founded on principles of honor, duty, and service—guiding forces behind every mission, task, and challenge. In the military, individualism took a backseat to the mission. Success depended on teamwork, trust, and a steadfast commitment to the greater good. Serving abroad broadened my worldview. As a soldier stationed overseas, I was exposed to different cultures, and the military base became a melting pot of nationalities and backgrounds. This environment constantly reminded me of the global nature of our work and the interconnectedness of our world. The armed forces were not just serving the United States. However, they were part of an international coalition committed to maintaining peace and security in an increasingly volatile world. This realization added another layer of significance to my service. Every drill, mission, and task contributed to a more significant effort to uphold the values of freedom and stability worldwide.

In Germany, I found a renewed sense of purpose. My time in uniform grounded me and reaffirmed my initial motivations for enlisting. The discipline, camaraderie, and knowledge we contributed to something larger than ourselves brought immense fulfillment. Knowing my work as a soldier mattered—contributing to a mission of significance each day—gave me clarity and direction.

Looking ahead, I recognized that my career was truly beginning. The tests I faced during basic training prepared me for adversity's rigors. But my time in Germany taught me something even more valuable: adaptability, discipline, and purpose would guide me through whatever lay ahead. Whether in a conflict zone or back home, the lessons I learned would serve me well as a soldier and an individual. This chapter wasn't just about training; it was about embracing the role of service and understanding that being a soldier meant contributing to something far beyond my ambitions. It was about safeguarding the values I held dear and ensuring their protection for the future.

Deployment, however, was a stark reminder of the harsh realities of war. While training had equipped me for various tests, the unpredictability of war demanded a level of constant vigilance that no drill could replicate. Each day brought new hurdles, and while physical dangers loomed large, it was the emotional and psychological toll that tested me the most. The mental strain of living in a conflict zone—where every movement could mean the difference between life and death—was something I couldn't fully grasp until I experienced it firsthand.

War reduces life to its essential elements: survival, solidarity, and purpose. Every decision carried tremendous weight; even the slightest mistake could have profound consequences. The camaraderie built during basic training took on new meaning during deployment. The bonds I shared with my fellow soldiers became our lifeline. We relied on each other for stability, encouragement, and, most importantly, trust. The friendships forged through adversity became unbreakable, and it was clear that our success—and survival—depended on our ability to function as a cohesive unit. We had trained for this moment, and those bonds united us in the face of real danger.

I vividly remember a night in the operations center in Mannheim. The room hummed with the low buzz of radios and the glow of computer screens, casting a different kind of tension in the air. Every incoming transmission felt significant; each status report reminded us that our work had real-life consequences for those on the frontlines. The weight of that responsibility sat heavily on my shoulders— knowing that even a minor communication lapse could disrupt critical missions. Yet, in the quiet moments between transmissions, I found comfort in the camaraderie of my team. We were thousands of miles from the battlefield, but we were in this together, and that shared purpose gave us strength.

These reflections grounded me, reinforcing the belief that our presence and sacrifices contributed to something larger than ourselves. Despite adversity, I found strength in knowing that our work made a tangible difference in the lives of those affected by war. This sense of purpose sustained me through the most challenging days, constantly reminding me that the mission was worth the fight despite the harsh realities of deployment.

In 2003, I stationed in Mannheim, Germany, with the 5th Signal Command, known as the "Dragon Warriors." Our unit played a critical role in ensuring the functionality of communication systems vital for mission command-and-control operations. While many of our comrades deployed to Iraq, our mission in Mannheim was no less critical. We were responsible for ensuring seamless communication, logistical support, and the functionality of essential systems, enabling those on the frontlines to carry out their operations precisely and efficiently. Although we were far from direct action, our work connected commanders to their troops.

The Mannheim area was a hub of U.S. defense forces activity, constantly buzzing with tasks focused on operational readiness. Every message that passed through our systems was strategically important, from satellite communications to troubleshooting tactical radios. We understand that even minor disruptions could have dire consequences, potentially risking lives or hampering critical missions. The responsibility we shouldered was immense, and we took it seriously, knowing the success of our comrades depended on our precision and efficiency.

Yet, rear deployment came with its emotional challenges. While those deployed to Iraq faced immediate physical dangers, we grappled with the emotional complexity of watching the war unfold from thousands of miles away. The distance created a strange duality: immense pride in knowing our work was essential but also a lingering frustration and disconnect from the dangers our comrades faced. News of casualties and battle updates served as a harsh reminder of the realities of war, even as we fulfilled our vital mission from afar.

This sense of isolation magnified the emotional toll of rear deployment. We knew our work was crucial, but the separation from direct combat sometimes made it difficult to reconcile our sense of purpose with the intensity of the conflict. We were fighting the same war but in different ways. Our camaraderie became our anchor during these times as we leaned on one another for support, understanding that the mental toughness we faced was just as significant as the physical ones. Rear deployment was not just about managing logistics; it was about maintaining mental resilience in a charged and emotionally distant environment.

2006: Guarding U.S. Sites in Germany

## ADAPTING TO SHIFTING ROLES

As my time in Mannheim, Germany, ended, I witnessed a profound shift in the presence of U.S. power across the region. Once-bustling bases in central Germany, including Heidelberg, were gradually phased out as part of a broader realignment of U.S. forces in Europe. Operations began consolidating in southern Germany, particularly around the Nuremberg area. What was once a vibrant base hub slowly transformed into a quiet, almost deserted outpost, marking the end of an era for Mannheim and those of us who served there.

Reflecting on my time with the 5th Signal Command, I recognized our critical role. While we were not on the front lines, our work in maintaining communication systems and providing logistical support was vital to the success of those who were. This realignment symbolized the closure of Mannheim's chapter in U.S. history, underscoring the lasting impact of our efforts. Ironically, many buildings that once housed this military power have been repurposed into refugee housing. Seeing these facilities now providing shelter and safety for displaced people fills me with deep pride. What once symbolized U.S. strength has now become a beacon of hope.

## TRANSITIONING INTO CIVILIAN LIFE

After my honorable discharge, I quickly realized that transitioning into civilian life was not as straightforward as I had hoped. Despite the skills and discipline gained in the military, finding a job proved challenging. My role primarily in logistics—did not directly align with many civilian job opportunities. Employers struggled to see how my experience translated to their workforce needs. It became clear that I needed to upgrade my qualifications to compete in the civilian job market.

This realization led me to return to school, where I pursued degrees in computer science and cybersecurity— fields that demanded a different skill set than I had developed while in uniform. This marked a transformative career shift, redefining how my abilities could thrive in a new environment. Though the transition was challenging, it ultimately opened doors to opportunities I had never imagined.

## NAVIGATING VETERAN HEALTHCARE

Near the end of my service, I began experiencing medical issues that marked the beginning of a long and arduous journey. Despite these life-changing ordeals, I was determined to fulfill my responsibilities to my comrades and complete my mission. There were days when the pain was unbearable, but I pushed through, driven by a deep sense of duty.

However, transitioning into civilian life meant not only finding employment but also navigating a medical system that often seemed ill-equipped to address the unique needs of veterans. The VA, overwhelmed by the influx of returning service members, struggled to keep pace with the demand for medical care. Veterans waited months—or even years—for treatment. Some, unable to receive the care they needed, found themselves homeless, mentally and physically broken by a system that had failed them.

I was fortunate enough to receive timely care from the VA. However, in 2016, I encountered a disturbing issue when seeking treatment from a VA-approved provider. The provider informed me they no longer accept VA patients due to payment delays. "The VA doesn't pay us on time," they said. "It takes too long to get reimbursed, and we can't afford to keep serving their patients."

It was a wake-up call. If I, someone who had received relatively timely care, faced such obstacles, what were other veterans experiencing? This experience highlighted just how deeply flawed the system was. Fortunately, the VA MISSION Act, passed around this time, introduced changes that allowed veterans to access healthcare beyond VA facilities, making it easier to see local providers. While the system remains imperfect, this law represented a meaningful step forward in improving access to care.

## REFLECTIONS ON THE VA REFORMS

In recent years, significant efforts have been made to reform the VA and improve veterans' access to care. While challenges remain, these reforms mark meaningful progress. The VA MISSION Act of 2018 expanded healthcare options beyond VA facilities, simplifying the process for veterans to receive care from local providers. Additional resources were allocated, and technological improvement was implemented to enhance the system's ability to track and manage appointments. These changes, though imperfect, have made a significant difference in improving access to care for many veterans.

Amidst these challenges, one constant source of strength was the enduring bond I shared with a comrade I had helped adjust to our unit. Years earlier, when he was reassigned to our team, I made it my mission to ensure he felt supported. The camaraderie we built during that time solidified our connection, and we've remained close ever since. He served over twenty years and was honorably retired. Little did I know that the support I offered him back then would one day come into full circle, as he provided me with the same strength when I navigated the complexities of the VA healthcare system.

His insight and mentorship guided me through the bureaucratic maze of veterans' care, and his support reminded me that the bonds forged in service transcend the battlefield. These relationships became a lifeline as I faced the uncertainties of civilian life. Whether solving immediate issues, planning new ventures, or reminiscing about shared experiences, these connections remain invaluable.

A former supervisor who has remained steadfastly supportive throughout the years further exemplified the enduring nature of these relationships. When I reached out for a recommendation during my graduate school application, he generously provided a thoughtful reference that helped secure my acceptance. Even after all these years, his willingness to support me reflects the deep bonds we formed while serving our country.

2003 Fort Knox, Kentucky, Completion of Army Basic
Training with comrade

## Chapter 4: REDEFINING PURPOSE

After years of active duty and reservist, the obstacles of transitioned back to civilian activities, I discovered that my path was shaped not only by a sense of duty but also by passions that fueled my purpose. The shift from the military to the civilian side is never straightforward; it requires resilience, patience, and a willingness to reinvent oneself while holding onto the values learned in uniform. Some of the core values I developed during my army time—discipline, perseverance, and a strong work ethic—became the foundation on which I built a new, meaningful life. However, what inspired and drove me were my passions: faith, technology, family, travel, and wellness. These interests became the pillars that helped me navigate the complexities of post-service living, leading to personal growth, healing, and a renewed sense of vision.

Faith played a critical role during and after my career. In the face of adversity and the emotional strain that comes with service, my faith served as a steady source of strength. It provided the guidance I needed to remain grounded amidst uncertainty. My faith offered stability through the

91

most challenging moments, reassuring me when everything around me felt chaotic. After leaving the military, this faith continued to anchor me as I adjusted to the civilian lifestyle, allowing me to reflect on my experiences, make sense of my ordeals, and move forward with gratitude. More than personal courage, my faith became a community where I connected with others who shared my values and experiences, easing the loneliness that often accompanies transitioning out of the tour of duty.

After all that, I discovered a passion for technology that opened new doors for personal and professional growth. While my role focused on logistics and supplies, I felt an undeniable pull toward computer science after transitioning toward civilian. This trek began with earning a bachelor's degree in computer science, which provided me with a solid technical foundation and ignited my curiosity about the rapidly evolving digital landscape. I later pursued a master's degree in cybersecurity engineering, gaining specialized knowledge in protecting systems and defending against cyber threats.

The discipline, attention to detail, and problem-solving skills I developed during that time translated seamlessly into my studies and my work in cybersecurity. I became

92

fascinated by how technology connects people, reshapes industries, and fortifies global security. This career allowed me to continue serving society, this time by safeguarding critical infrastructures and protecting sensitive data. My experience and formal Education gave me a new sense of mission—one that I was eager to carry forward.

Travel also became a profound source of personal healing and inspiration. I was exposed to unfamiliar cultures, landscapes, and perspectives across the globe, sparking an endured exploration. After leaving the army, travel became a way to continue getting rid of new places and within myself. Each trip offered opportunities for reflection and growth. I also learned languages such as Arabic, German, and Spanish.

Whether visiting familiar or foreign destinations, travel allowed me to step outside the structured world and embrace new perspectives on it, humanity, and my place there. It provided space to heal from past unpleasant experiences, find peace in nature and culture, and develop a deeper understanding of the interconnectedness of all people.

Physical and mental wellness became another important. After years of physical and mental demands in uniform, I began to appreciate the importance of self-care. Wellness evolved from merely staying fit into a holistic practice focused on nurturing my emotional and spiritual well-being. Exercise, mindfulness, and a commitment to overall health allowed me to heal from the visible and invisible scars that I had left behind. Wellness became essential in my reintegration into civilian life, helping me manage stress, build resilience, and find balance in a world without the structured demands of the past.

Reflecting on my path from duty to civilian flow, I recognize that my passions—technology, family, travel, and well-being—have been instrumental in shaping who I am today. They haven't just helped me survive the transition and enabled me to thrive within it. Faith kept me grounded, technology sparked my professional growth, travel broadened my horizons, and wellness gave me the courage to care for myself sustainably. These passions have created a path forward, leading me to personal growth, healing, and a renewed sense of purpose.

This chapter of my journey is marked by the mission I once served and the passions that emerged in its wake. These passions have guided me through civilian life with resilience, curiosity, and a steadfast commitment to ongoing self-discovery.

## REFLECTING ON THE JOURNEY

The aftermath of 9/11 and the subsequent "Operation Enduring Freedom" came with immense costs—both financial and human—leading many to question the broader implications of the war. While the mission to eliminate Osama bin Laden was ultimately successful, the long-term effects of the conflict continue to shape American policies and the lives of those who served. Operation Enduring Freedom was initially launched as a decisive response to global terrorism. However, it evolved into a prolonged and costly engagement. While its immediate objectives—dismantling al-Qaeda and capturing Osama bin Laden—were achieved, the conflict's enduring repercussions have left profound scars on the nation and those who served.

As an immigrant, a soldier, and someone who has witnessed political instability firsthand, I understand the toll of war on a profoundly personal level. The weight of war, displacement, and the overwhelming responsibility of caring for my family has left lasting marks—both visible and hidden. For much of my existence, I carried these burdens quietly, pushing through pain and hardship without fully addressing the emotional toll they took on me. The distress of fleeing conflict, enduring the chaos of refugee life, and serving during global unrest compounded my internal fights. At times, the stress and concern felt unbearable yet admitting that I needed help seemed even more difficult. Like many others who have experienced war and displacement, I grappled with the emotional aftermath long after the physical dangers had passed. The memories of conflict, loss, and the weight of responsibility often felt insurmountable.

Coming to terms with the impact of these experiences on my overall health was a slow and humble process, but it was necessary for my survival. I began my journey toward healing through therapy, support groups, and spiritual guidance. Addressing my core issues didn't come quickly; it required confronting the fears and emotions I had long suppressed. However, in facing those fights, I discovered the energy that comes from vulnerability. One of the hardest lessons was realizing that health ordeals are not a sign of weakness—seeking help that requires incredible courage. This process taught me to be more compassionate toward myself and others. By sharing my experiences, I hope to break the stigma surrounding veterans' health concerns, particularly for those who have faced the difficulties of war and displacement.

Healing is not a single event but a continuous process that requires patience, self-reflection, and the willingness to seek help. Reflecting on my journey, I've understood that asking for support is not a sign of weakness but an act of energy. I want others to face similar obstacles to know they are not alone. Although the trauma of war and displacement may leave deep scars, with the proper support, healing is always possible. By opening about my painful experiences, I hope to inspire others to seek help and continue their healing journey with resilience and determination.

As someone who fled conflict in Ethiopia and found a new home in the United States, I have witnessed the acute impact that war and peace can have on people's lives. At the age of fourteen, I left Ethiopia, a homeland engulfed in the chaos of a brutal civil war, torn apart by deep ideological divides and relentless violence. This experience shaped my understanding of how polarization can fracture a nation and or improve the lives of its citizens. In many ways, it allows me to view American politics through a unique lens that recognizes both the opportunities within a functioning democracy and the dangers that arise when division goes unchecked.

Growing up in Ethiopia's Tigray region, I saw firsthand the devastating consequences of a divided society. Political instability and ethnic tensions escalated into violence, turning neighbors against each other and forcing countless families, including my own, to flee for safety. Witnessing communities unravel due to ideological differences taught me that peace and stability are fragile treasures that require constant effort to uphold. Those turbulent years instilled a deep understanding of the importance of unity, cooperation, and resilience—values that have since become unwavering pillars guiding my life.

When I first arrived in the United States, I viewed democracy as a beacon of hope. In this system, different perspectives could coexist and work toward the common good. In my early days of learning about American politics, I was optimistic about the promise of collaboration and compromise. However, I noticed a growing divide over time, much like other countries. The political system I admired from far was fracturing, with both major parties entrenched in their positions and unwilling to work together. Just as divisions tore through Ethiopia, the polarization in American politics could carry dangerous consequences, threatening the foundation of a society built on diversity and the exchange of ideas.

Watching this unfold, I reflect on how fragile political systems can be—whether in a developing country like Ethiopia or a global superpower like the United States. The rise of partisan media and misinformation only deepens these divides, much like propaganda fueled tensions in my homeland. Political rhetoric, used as a weapon, fosters an "us versus them" mentality that tears at the social fabric. In America, polarization is more than just political disagreement; it represents a deeper issue of identity, culture, and trust. Just as the communities I grew up in fell apart due to unresolved political conflict, I fear the same fate could transpire in America if the current trajectory continues unchecked.

Reflecting on my journey, I've understood that resilience is not merely about enduring conflict; it's about taking purposeful steps to heal divisions and rebuilding what has been broken. During my time in the army, I learned the importance of teamwork, collaboration, and unity. We were united by a shared mission, regardless of our backgrounds or political beliefs. That sense of unity was paramount to our success and survival. It's a lesson that resonates deeply with me as I observe how the increasing polarization in American politics starkly contrasts the principles I learned while serving.

In the military, we couldn't afford division; we had to trust each other and work together despite our differences. The gridlock and division in American politics threaten the unity I once fought to protect.

The system of checks and balances, designed to safeguard the interests of all Americans, has become strained under the weight of partisanship. Reflecting on my sacrifice, I see the defense force as a model for what American society could be—diverse individuals working together for a common goal. The lessons I learned there about unity, cooperation, and resilience apply to the battlefield and the political arena.

At a time of increasing division, America must remember the force of working together, regardless of differences. Resilience in political division requires a commitment to dialogue, compromise, and a shared sense of responsibility for the nation's future. It's not enough to survive political gridlock; we must actively strive to heal divisions and rebuild the trust that holds our democracy together. By fostering collaboration and seeking common ground, America can overcome the challenges of polarization and build a more unified, resilient future.

Authentic leadership is not measured by power but by the capacity to serve others with integrity and compassion. Throughout history, the most impactful leaders—like Nelson Mandela—did not rise to prominence through force but by embodying the principles of justice, empathy, and a genuine desire to transform society for the better. In today's increasingly interconnected world, authentic global leadership is more crucial than ever, and the call for social justice has become increasingly urgent. Leaders today face many complex challenges—inequality, climate change, migration, and conflict among them. Addressing these issues demands not only collaboration on a global scale but also a steadfast commitment to fairness and equity.

Unfortunately, political leaders often act out of self-interest, neglecting the marginalized while prioritizing short-term gains. However, the most influential leaders use their platform to champion human rights, bridge divides, and advocate for justice.

Social justice demands leaders who uphold every individual's inherent dignity and courage to confront entrenched systems of inequality and discrimination. Authentic leadership goes beyond political posturing, addressing the more profound, systemic issues that sustain inequity. It calls on nations to combat poverty, protect the environment, and guarantee universal access to Education and healthcare. We can build a more just and equitable world through sustained and collaborative efforts.

Reflecting on my journey—from witnessing political instability and social unrest in Ethiopia to building a future in the United States—I have seen firsthand the profound need for principled leadership. We need leaders driven not by political gain but by the values of fairness, empathy, and justice. We need leaders who do not merely react to crises but proactively work to address the root causes of injustice, creating systems that uplift the vulnerable and build more inclusive societies. This type of leadership, rooted in service and driven by principles rather than politics, will guide future generations toward a world where justice is not just an ideal but a reality.

## EDUCATION A PATH TO REDEMPTION

As I embarked on the challenging path of adjusting to it in the United States, the classroom became more than just a space for academic learning—it transformed into my sanctuary, my refuge. Amid the chaos of navigating a new culture, overcoming language barriers, and reconciling my past with an uncertain future, the classroom offered me a sense of structure and control. Surrounded by textbooks and lessons, I could temporarily set aside the trials of my past and imagine a future beyond the hardships of being a refugee and a foster child. Each lesson represented an opportunity to build a life I had only dared to dream of during my quietest, most hopeful moments in Sudan.

Nevertheless, the language barrier proved to be my greatest challenge. Each day became a struggle, not only with the subject matter but with the words themselves. Understanding the language around me felt daunting, yet rather than allowing it to overwhelm me, I used it to fuel my determination. I quickly realized that my will to learn outweighed my fear of failure. Clinging to Nelson Mandela's words "Education is the most powerful weapon you can use to change the world," I found a personal mantra that resonated deeply. Education was not merely a tool for survival but a key to unlocking doors that had been closed by war, displacement, and self-imposed limitations. It could lead me beyond my current obstacles and toward a brighter, more hopeful future.

Education became my anchor in foster care, grounding me with purpose during uncertainty. Even before arriving in the United States, I understood that knowledge was my way out using rising above the chaos that had defined much of my life. The consistency and stability I found in the classroom, even as I moved between foster homes, provided a foundation I could rely on. It was a space where I could focus on building a future defined not by my past but by my aspirations. My commitment to education deepened when I settled in with a new foster family. Their unwavering support helped me see Education as a survival tool and a source of empowerment, something that could change my outlook and shape how I engaged with the world. I realized that Education was not just about acquiring knowledge but about the power it gave me to redefine my narrative.

My foster family played an essential role in nurturing my educational path. They understood how vital Education was to me and supported my ambitions wholeheartedly.

Their encouragement was constant. They believed in me even when I struggled to believe in myself, attending every school event and parent-teacher conference and celebrating every milestone, no matter how small. Their faith in my potential pushed me to aim higher and dream bigger. With their support, I began to see Education as more than a pathway to personal success; it became a means to build a soul. I could be proud of—one not limited by my past but shaped by my future potential.

Yet, Education was not my only source of energy. Every Sunday, I found comfort in the church. My faith became a vital part of my resilience, offering spiritual grounding that complemented the intellectual growth I was experiencing in the classroom. Though the worlds of foster care and the church may have seemed distinct, they felt interconnected to me. Just as my foster family provided stability and love, the church offered a more profound sense of spiritual belonging.

It was a place where I could reflect on my future path and find comfort in believing that all my hardships had a purpose. The church became another refuge, giving me the energy to face the uncertainties that shaped my path. Within its walls, I learned the importance of faith—not only in

God but in myself—and this belief empowered me to confront the tests of my new spirit with renewed purpose.

Both the classroom and the church provided communities that believed in me. Whether it was my foster parents pushing me to excel academically or my church community offering spiritual encouragement, I realized that I was not alone on this path. My resilience was not just about surviving foster care or adapting to a new country; it was about embracing every opportunity for growth and allowing those around me to support and guide me through the challenges I faced. The unwavering support of these two communities empowered me to thrive in ways I never imagined, reminding me that my past does not define me— my choices do. Their belief in me strengthened my self-confidence, teaching me that Education was a means of survival and a powerful tool to build a future rooted in growth and possibility.

History and English interest me the most among the subjects I studied. History became a source of comfort as I explored the lives of people who had faced adversity, seeing reflections of my journey in their stories. The accounts of revolutions, social movements, and the resilience of the human spirit were not merely lessons in

106

the past; they were reminders that hardship is universal. History taught me that adversity can be conquered, providing comfort in understanding that my challenges were part of a greater narrative of human resilience and perseverance.

As I gained fluency in English, words became a new power source. They allowed me to express my thoughts, hopes, and dreams in ways I had never encountered before. Each essay and story I wrote marked a new part of myself—one no longer bound by the past but open to future possibilities. Language became my means of connecting with the world around me, helping me find my place and articulate my identity in a new land.

As my understanding of history and language deepened, I began to see Education as a tool not just for personal growth but for responsibility. The knowledge I was gaining was not only for my benefit; it was something I could use to help others face their tests. I started viewing myself as a student and as someone who could contribute to my community, utilizing Education as a force for good. This realization transformed my perspective, revealing that Education was not solely about achieving my goals but about using what I had learned to impact the world positively. I can complete any forms and other applications independently without needing assistance from others.

Mastering English has been crucial in creating a smoother, less stressful, significantly boosting my self-esteem. Education became more than just a means to an end; it became a core part of my identity. It gave me the strength to move forward and imagine a future defined not by my past but by my actions, perseverance, and commitment to growth. Education has been, and continues to be, the beacon that has carried me through some of the most challenging moments of my life. It is the foundation upon which I've built everything that followed. Education opened a path forward, giving me a sense of purpose and belonging that enabled me to thrive, dream, and grow into the person I am destined to become.

When I first arrived in the United States, the digital landscape was in its infancy. Smartphones were a rarity, apps were non-existent, and technology played a significantly smaller role daily. Since then, technology has profoundly transformed how we live, mainly how we communicate. What once required letters or landlines can now be achieved instantly through apps, connecting people across continents in seconds.

Technology has revolutionized communication and strengthened global security, equipping nations with advanced tools to prevent threats and maintain stability. However, these advancements bring their challenges. The rise of digital surveillance and the widespread collection of personal data have raised concerns about privacy and ethics. Balancing the need for security with protecting individual rights has become more critical than ever.

Modern society has evolved into an interconnected world, where ideas and information can be exchanged in real-time, regardless of distance. In global security, technology offers powerful tools for intelligence gathering and defense. However, it also presents ethical dilemmas, as the misuse of personal data threatens individual freedoms. Striking a balance between safeguarding security and preserving privacy is essential to maintaining trust in this increasingly digital age.

My fascination with technology began in childhood. Even at a young age, I was captivated by computers and the intricate systems powering them. I would spend hours disassembling old machines, marveling at how each component worked harmoniously to bring a device to life. Watching a machine operate, with its hardware and

109

software working together seamlessly, felt almost magical. This early curiosity sparked a lifelong passion for technology, which has remained central to my life and career. Even then, I sensed the vast potential of technology—not just as a tool for solving complex problems but as a bridge to new worlds of possibility.

This passion for technology stayed with me throughout adulthood. It became pivotal in my transition from uniform duty to civilian life. After leaving the military, I sought something that could provide both intellectual challenge and personal fulfillment. Technology offered me that opportunity, no longer just a hobby, and it became my way to re-engage with the world and reintegrate into civilians. The dynamic, fast-paced nature of the tech industry mirrored the energy and adaptability I had cultivated in the military, making it a natural fit for my post-service career. Technology became more than just an interest; it evolved into a career path where I could continue to find purpose, drawing on the discipline, precision, and problem-solving skills I acquired in uniform.

Driven to transform this passion into a professional career, I began exploring various fields within technology. I enrolled in online courses, immersing myself in cybersecurity, coding, and systems management. I found the structure and discipline required in these fields compelling—qualities I had grown accustomed to in the military. Programming, for example, demanded the same precision and attention to detail as the operations, while cybersecurity necessitated vigilance and foresight, much like the strategic thinking required on the battlefield. These disciplines felt familiar yet presented new challenges that excited and motivated me. The more I learned, the more I realized that technology gave me a sense of mission and focus that resonated with my unique experience.

As I delved deeper into the world of technology, I discovered something I hadn't fully anticipated: the creativity it allowed. Coding was not just about following instructions; it was about innovation, problem-solving, and creating something entirely new. I found immense satisfaction in troubleshooting issues and developing systems that operated flawlessly. The intellectual challenge of solving complex problems reignited the sense of purpose I had experienced during my enlisted years. Once tasked with logistical and tactical challenges in the field, I was now addressing technical issues in a data-driven world. Technology became my new mission, and I approached it with the same dedication and determination that had defined my duty. Most of my Education is acquired through self-thought from reading or online research.

The discipline I gained from that experience translated seamlessly into my pursuit of a career in technology. I approached every course, certification, and professional milestone with the same work ethic that had carried me through basic training and deployment. I earned certifications in cybersecurity, attended workshops, and joined professional communities to learn from others and sharpen my skills. The structured nature of uniform service, emphasizing order, continual improvement, and adaptability, provided the foundation I needed to excel in the tech sector. Each new skill I acquired felt like another step toward mastering a field that challenged and inspired me. Technology was no longer just a passion; it had become a vocation.

Eventually, my passion for technology culminated in a career in cybersecurity, where I discovered a deep sense of purpose. In many ways, cybersecurity felt like a continuation of it. Just as I had once been responsible for safeguarding my fellow soldiers and ensuring the success of operations, I now found myself tasked with protecting

112

individuals and organizations from malicious electronic threats. The mission had evolved, but the core objective was to protect and defend. Cybersecurity demanded the same attention to detail, vigilance, and strategic thinking I had developed in the military. I embraced these challenges with enthusiasm.

Each project I undertook in cybersecurity reminded me of my direction. Whether I was securing networks, analyzing threats, or developing strategies to protect sensitive information, I understood that my work had real-world implications. Cybersecurity was solving technical problems, safeguarding livelihoods, securing critical infrastructures, and maintaining trust in our digital systems. In this way, technology allowed me to continue serving, though in a different capacity. The sense of responsibility I had as a soldier was now embedded in my work as a cybersecurity professional, imparting a purpose to my career beyond personal achievement.

Technology became more than just a career; it became a way to stay connected to the values that had shaped me throughout. The discipline, resilience, and problem-solving skills I had developed in the service found a new outlet in the tech world. Just as my service had brought me pride and fulfillment, so did my cybersecurity work. Every challenge I overcame, every system I secured, and every issue I resolved reminded me that I was making a difference— protecting the digital spaces where people live, work, and connect. Technology is not solely about innovation or advancement; it's about serving a greater purpose. That purpose continues to drive me forward today.

While technology stimulated my intellectual and professional ambitions, travel became essential to my healing path after the military. I traveled extensively during my years of service, but those trips were regimented and focused on official duties. In the military, there was little opportunity to experience the culture or environment around me. After leaving, I felt an undeniable urge to travel—not out of duty or obligation, but fueled by curiosity, a thirst for adventure, and the desire for personal growth. Travel became my pathway to healing and self-discovery, allowing me to break free from the structured world I had known and reconnect with myself on a deeper level.

Each crossing became a form of therapy, a way to escape the daily demands and find peace in unfamiliar surroundings. Stepping into new environments helped me

114

reflect on experiences with fresh eyes. Whether I was wandering the charming streets of Heidelberg, exploring the vibrant cityscape of Paris, or walking through the historic neighborhoods of San Jose, Costa Rica, each place offered a new perspective on the world and me. Unlike that, where orders dictated every move, travel presented an open canvas where each decision led to new experiences, perspectives, and insights.

Heidelberg provided a serene setting for self-reflection, with its picturesque old town hugging the Neckar River. The centuries-old architecture, crowned by the majestic Heidelberg Castle, invited me to slow down and reconnect with history. Walking along the Philosopher's Walk—a scenic path that had inspired poets and thinkers—I felt deeply connected to the beauty around me.

The tranquility of Heidelberg stood in stark contrast to the intensity of the armed forces, giving me space to process my travel thus far. The city's peaceful atmosphere reminded me that living is about pushing forward and taking moments to pause, reflect, and appreciate the quiet beauty surrounding us.

Frankfurt, on the other hand, offered a different kind of experience. As Germany's financial hub, the city pulsed with energy and modernity. Skyscrapers towered over the skyline yet nestled amidst them stood historic landmarks like Römer Square and the Gothic Bartholomew's mew's Cathedral. Frankfurt is constantly composed of the city's seamless blend of the old and the new. The fast-paced environment inspired me to embrace constant evolution— just as Frankfurt had rebuilt itself after wartime destructive, I was rebuilding myself. The city's energy fueled my desire to move forward, embrace change, and trust that renewal is always possible, even after periods of upheaval.

Mannheim, with its mix of industry, history, and culture, offered a new layer of reflection. Having been stationed there during my time in the military, returning as a civilian marked a pivotal moment in my transformation. The city's grid-like streets and baroque architecture once symbolized structure and purpose during my service, yet now I saw them through a fresh perspective. Mannheim's blend of resilience and renewal mirrored my own journey.

As I walked through its familiar streets, I felt the weight of my past experiences, but I also recognized how far I had come in my personal growth. What was once a symbol of duty becoming an integral part of my healing process.

116

As I traveled, I began conversing with people in German, Spanish, and Arabic—languages I had picked up. Speaking another language enhanced communication and transformed my perspective. It opened doors to deeper connections, providing a richer understanding of the cultures around me. Conversations with locals revealed insights into their lives, histories, and worldviews. The ability to communicate in their language fostered a sense of belonging, allowing me to see beyond my own experiences and deepen my connection to those I encountered.

Traveling through these cities helped me confront parts of myself that I set aside during my time. While survival demanded it, the rigid structure of it often left little room for personal exploration or vulnerability. Travel, by contrast, encouraged me to embrace uncertainty, take risks, and trust the process of discovery.

As I navigated foreign cultures, language barriers, and unfamiliar landscapes, I realized that not everything could be controlled or predicted perfectly. These experiences brought a new resilience that complemented the discipline I had learned there while adding a softer, more revealed Heidelberg to Frankfurter.

Heidelberg's calm, Mannheim's vibrant energy, and Mannheim's significance all contributed to my route of rediscovery. Each trip allowed me to revisit the past in healing rather than painful ways. It gave me the distance I needed to reflect on the experiences that had shaped me, both the challenges and rewards, and how those experiences continued to influence my present and future.

Through these travels, I understood that self-discovery is an ongoing process. Travel allowed me to explore unfamiliar places and new facets of my personality and soul. I found joy in spontaneity, resilience in discomfort, and growth in the challenges of navigating unfamiliar territories. The lessons from travel were not always easy, but they were profound. Patience in the face of language barriers, adaptability in unpredictable circumstances, and the ability to find common ground with strangers deepened my understanding of myself and my place in the world.

Travel became more than a way to see unfamiliar places; it became a critical part of my healing process. It allowed me to shed the armor I had worn for so long and approach living with an open heart and mind. Boundaries, rules, and orders no longer defined the world—they became a space of infinite possibility, where each path led to new insights,

118

and each destination brought me closer to understanding who I was. Through travel, I rediscovered myself—not as a soldier or a civilian, but as someone continually evolving, shaped by my past and the new horizons I was yet to explore.

While technology and travel stimulated my mind and soul, wellness became essential to maintaining service and mental health. My service's rigorous physical and emotional demands undoubtedly took a toll on me. As I transitioned into civilian, I realized I needed to prioritize my well-being in ways I didn't. It conditioned me to push through pain, suppress emotional strain, and compartmentalize stress to stay focused. Post-service experience, however, required a different approach involving holistically nurturing my body, mind, and spirit. Wellness became a trek toward balance, healing, self-awareness, and overall health.

Physical fitness, a crucial part of my regimen, took on new meaning as I embraced wellness. Instead of focusing solely on energy and stamina, I began to view fitness to enhance my mental clarity and emotional well-being. Exercise transformed from an obligation into an act of self-care. I incorporated various forms of movement into my daily routine—not out of necessity but as a conscious choice to nurture my body and mind. Running, cycling, and yoga became integral to my day, offering unique benefits that helped me balance.

Walking, for example, became a powerful outlet for releasing pent-up energy and tension. There was something meditative about the rhythmic pounding of my feet on the pavement, the steady breathing, and the sense of freedom that came with moving through space. Walking day clears my mind, processes the day's events, and channels stress into something constructive. It grounded me, reconnecting my body and mind while offering solitude amidst busyness. Running was a physical and emotional release, enabling me to decompress and build resilience simultaneously.

Cycling, on the other hand, provided a sense of adventure and exploration. It allowed me to connect with the world around me exhilaratingly and freely. As I rode through new neighborhoods, parks, and countryside trails, I felt the thrill of discovery that paralleled my travels. Cycling urged me to be present, appreciate my surroundings, and embrace the joy of movement. It provided physical accomplishment along with the emotional rewards of exploration and self-discovery.

120

Yoga introduced a gentler, more mindful approach to wellness. Unlike the high-intensity activities of running or cycling, yoga encouraged me to slow down, breathe deeply, and be fully present. Through yoga, I cultivated mindfulness, developing a deeper awareness of my body and its needs. It offered a chance to release tension built up over years of physical and emotional strain, enabling me to embrace relaxation without guilt. Yoga became not just physical practice but a tool for managing stress, reducing anxiety, and promoting mental clarity. The combination of movement and meditation within yoga provided a holistic approach to well-being, reminding me that caring for my physical health was intrinsically linked to my mental and emotional wellness.

Beyond physical activity, mindfulness practices like meditation have become essential to my wellness routine. My enlisted years left little room for introspection of life's emotional processing. It was life's fast-paced, high-stakes nature that allowed little space for personal reflection. As I transitioned into civilian life, however, I realized that the emotions and anxieties I had compartmentalized needed to be addressed. Meditation offered the space to confront these feelings directly, allowing me to sit with them and process them in a way that fostered inner peace.

Regular meditation taught me to quiet my mind, observe my thoughts with detachment, and find calm amidst life's chaos. During these moments of stillness, I found the clarity I had been seeking. Meditation became a practice of self-compassion, allowing me to acknowledge the complexities of my emotions and release the burdens I had carried from my experience, which wasn't.

It taught me that healing wasn't about erasing the past but accepting it, learning from it, and moving forward with a renewed sense of purpose. Much like yoga and meditation, it reminded me that wellness wasn't a luxury but a necessity, a foundational practice supporting every other aspect.

Wellness became a crossroad of self-care that extended far beyond physical fitness. It taught me the importance of nurturing every aspect of my health—body, mind, and spirit. Through exercise, mindfulness, and meditation, I learned to manage stress, alleviate anxiety, and sustainably find balance. Wellness became a daily practice, a commitment to myself that helped me maintain clarity, focus, and emotional stability. I understood that taking time for myself was not selfish but essential, especially after years of pushing through challenges without pausing to reflect or recharge.

Wellness became the cornerstone of my healing after service. It allowed me to reframe my approach to health, shifting from the endurance-driven mindset I had homed in the military to a more balanced, holistic understanding of what it truly means to thrive. I realized that strength was not just about physical power but about resilience, mindfulness, and the capacity to care for oneself in meaningful, lasting ways.

Through this journey toward wellness, I rediscovered a sense of balance that had long eluded me. It was about recovering from the physical toll and healing my mind and spirit. For years, I had relied on grit and perseverance to push through the challenges of my duty and the difficult transition to civilian life. But now, wellness has revealed a different path emphasizing nurturing the whole self. Yet, as I embraced this new way of living, I couldn't help but wonder: Could this balance withstand future adversity? I had come so far in pursuing well-being, but the unpredictability of life still loomed. Would the resilience I had cultivated be enough when new challenges inevitably arose? The answers, I knew, would come only with time. For now, wellness remains an essential part of my path, a foundation I continue to build, even as the unknown tests lie ahead. In every mission and every moment of doubt, I leaned on the power of God. Faith became my shield in moments of fear and my guide in moments of uncertainty. Through every difficulty, I knew that my military service had served a greater purpose, ordained by God's hand.

REDEFINING SUCCESS

Success is often equated with tangible achievements: prestigious job title, financial wealth, social status, or public recognition. These traditional measures of success are commonly celebrated in society. However, they don't necessarily reflect the full range of human potential or lead to genuine fulfillment. Redefining success means expanding our understanding beyond these narrow metrics, including personal well-being, emotional richness, and pursuing a life aligned with our values and purpose. True success, in this broader sense, lies in achieving fulfillment that is meaningful on a deeper, personal level.

One of the first steps in redefining success is to *question societal expectations.* We live in a world that often pressures us to conform to specific definitions of success— climbing that corporate ladder, accumulating material wealth, or seeking fame. But the truth is, these external measures do not necessarily add to happiness or a sense of fulfillment. They can sometimes create feelings of inadequacy or emptiness when we realize they do not align with values or bring lasting satisfaction. Redefining success

125

begins with recognizing that society's expectations do not bind societies. However, instead, we have the power to define success on our terms.

A key part of this process is identifying what *truly matters to us.* For some, success might mean achieving inner peace, fostering deep personal relationships, or living in a way that aligns with their moral values. It could involve pursuing a passion or creative endeavor, giving back to the community, or experiencing the world through travel and learning. When we focus on what is truly meaningful, success becomes more about the journey than the destination. Achieving personal fulfillment requires us to be in tune with our desires and make choices that support a life we genuinely want to live rather than one dictated by external pressures.

Additionally, redefining success requires a shift in our *perspective on failure.* In traditional measures of success, failure is often seen as something to avoid at all costs. This setback signals the end of the road. However, when redefining success, we see failure not as a permanent defeat but as an opportunity for growth. Failures are lessons, moments that push us to learn, adapt, and try again with more wisdom and experience. Instead of fearing failure, we

126

embrace it as a necessary part of the process that leads us to deeper understanding and more tremendous success in the long run.

Moreover, achieving fulfillment goes hand in hand with *self-compassion.* In pursuing success, many of us can become our harshest critics, constantly pushing ourselves toward higher achievements without acknowledging our progress. Redefining success means giving ourselves credit for our steps, celebrating small victories, and allowing ourselves grace along the way. The journey is just as important as the destination, and true success comes from recognizing and appreciating the effort and growth along the path, not just the result.

True fulfillment also comes from the understanding that success is not a fixed destination but *a dynamic process* that evolves. What we define as success in our twenties may shift as we grow older, which is okay. Redefining success means allowing ourselves the flexibility to adjust our goals and values as we experience new chapters in life. We do not need to stick down to one narrow definition of success; instead, we can evolve and adapt, seeking new forms of fulfillment that resonate with where we are in our journey.

127

Focusing on impact and contribution is a critical element of achieving fulfillment beyond traditional measures. Success is not just about what we achieve for ourselves but also about how we contribute to the world. Many find that the most meaningful sense of fulfillment comes from helping others through acts of kindness, mentorship, or dedicating time and resources to causes that matter. Success, in this broader sense, can be measured by the positive difference we make in the lives of others and the legacy we leave behind.

Ultimately, redefining success involves letting go of the societal pressures to conform to external standards and, instead, creating a meaningful life on our terms. It is about making incisional choices that reflect our values, pursuing passions that bring us joy, and embracing the flexibility to grow and evolve. True success is found in the alignment between who we are, what we do, and how we contribute to the world, fostering a sense of fulfillment far more prosperous and more enduring than traditional measures ever could be.

## Chapter 5: WINDOW TO THE PAST

UNDERSTANDING TIGRAI'S CONFLICTS

Though, I have built a life in the United States, my connection to Ethiopia and, more specifically, to Tigray- remains an integral part of my identity. For years, I hoped that my homeland had moved beyond its violent history and that the cycle of conflict had finally ended. But the resurgence of violence in Tigray in recent years has been a painful reminder that peace in Ethiopia has always been fragile and that the scars of past wars have never truly healed. In 2020, conflict erupted again with unimaginable brutality, rekindling the disturbance I endured during my childhood.

The situation in Tigray, Ethiopia, has been deeply tragic, marked by extreme violence, displacement, and widespread human suffering. The conflict, which began in late 2020 between the Tigray People Liberation Front (TPLF) and the Ethiopian government, escalated quickly and led to mass casualties, famine, and forced migration. Thousands of civilians have died because of direct violence, starvation, and the collapse of essential services. In stark contrast, tens

130

of thousands were displaced, seeking refuge within Ethiopia or across borders into neighboring countries like Sudan. The humanitarian crisis in the region was further exacerbated by widespread allegations of human rights abuses, including sexual violence, attacks on civilians, and the deliberate destruction of essential infrastructure.

This revision enhances the statement by providing additional detail and flow while maintaining the gravity of the situation. In 2021, U.S. Secretary of State Antony Blinken's description of the violence as 'ethnic cleansing' brought global attention to the scale of the atrocities. The term 'ethnic cleansing' specifically pointed to the targeted actions against certain ethnic groups. Yet, the suffering of other communities, including the Amhara and Oromos, was also integral to the broader conflict.

The international response has involved diplomatic pressure, sanctions, and calls for accountability. However, efforts to bring about a ceasefire and resolve the crisis have been slow and complicated—a peace agreement brokered by the African Union in November 2022 is seen as a step toward ending hostilities. However, the region remains deeply affected, with recovery expected to take years due to the extensive damage to human lives and infrastructure.

The situation in Tigray has underscored the urgent need for effective international intervention, humanitarian aid, and long-term efforts to ensure peace, justice, and healing for those who have suffered.

. This harsh reality has brought me back to the pain of my past, reminding me that the fight for peace, justice, and security in my homeland is far from over.

As I watch from afar, I see the same uncertainty and fear that once consumed my family now reflected in the faces of those forced to flee their homes. It is as though history is repeating itself, reminding me of the deep wounds that conflict leaves behind—wounds not quickly healed. Watching the conflict unfold in Tigray today feels like looking through a window into my past. The faces on the news, the stories of families torn apart by violence, they are not strangers to me. They are echoes of the environment I left behind. The fear gripping Tigray now is the same fear that gripped me as a child, unsure of what the next day would bring or whether my family would survive.

My journey from displacement to safety in the United States does not allow me to sit on the sidelines. The struggles of Tigray are my own, and the fight for peace is one I cannot ignore. Today, more than seventy thousand

Tigrayans are living in refugee camps in Sudan, just as I once did decades ago. Their lives are marked by hunger, uncertainty, and the overwhelming trauma of being exiled from their homes. These families, many of them women and children, endure harsh conditions with little hope of immediate relief. While international organizations like the United Nations and USAID provide essential resources, such as food, water, and shelter, the camps are no place for long-term living. The future for these refugees remains perilous, just as it did for me all those years ago.

Seeing history repeat itself compelled me to act. Together with others, we organized a grassroots effort to provide displaced civilians with scanty essentials like clothing, food, and medicine. Though the challenges were immense, our collective efforts temporarily relieved one hundred people in dire need. Yet, I knew that material aid alone could not address the full scope of the crisis. In addition to our work on the ground, I took our message to a larger stage. Partnering with major media outlets, I sought to amplify the stories of those affected by the conflict. I understood the critical importance of raising global awareness about the humanitarian crisis, using every platform available to emphasize the urgency of the situation

133

in Tigray. Through interviews and media coverage, I aimed to ensure that the world did not forget the people suffering in the region—just as they had once forgotten us.

For me, advocacy is not just about surviving the past; it is about using my experiences to fight for a better future for those still trapped in the cycle of violence. The conflict in Tigray has strengthened my commitment to ensuring that the voices of the displaced are heard and that their suffering does not go unnoticed. While our material aid can help ease immediate burdens, advocacy shines a spotlight on ongoing injustices, demanding the world respond.

Watching the conflict in Tigray unfold is a stark reminder that peace is fragile and fleeting. My journey has taught me that while we may find moments of safety, we can never forget the ongoing fight for justice. The past is not behind us; it lives on in the faces of those who continue to flee, suffer, and cling to hope for the peace they deserve. The fight for justice in Tigray is now my fight, and it will remain so if necessary.

Growing up in Ethiopia's Tigray region, I witnessed the devastating consequences of a divided society. Political instability and ethnic tensions escalated into violence, turning neighbors against one another and forcing countless

134

families, including myself, to flee for safety. Observing communities crumble due to ideological differences made me acutely aware of how fragile peace and stability can be. These early experiences taught me the importance of unity, cooperation, and resilience—values that have guided me throughout.

As someone who fled conflict in Ethiopia and found a new home in the United States, I have witnessed firsthand how deeply polarization can fracture a nation and uproot its citizens. When I left Ethiopia at the age of fourteen, my homeland was consumed by civil war, torn apart by ideological divides and violent conflict. This experience has shaped my understanding of the dangers of unchecked divisions. It allows me to view American politics through a unique lens, recognizing both the opportunities within a functioning democracy and the risks that arise when division festers.

Upon arriving in the United States, I saw democracy as a beacon of hope. In this system, differing perspectives could coexist and work toward the common good. In my early days of learning about American politics, I felt optimistic about the promise of collaboration and compromise. However, I noticed a growing divide over time, reminiscent

135

of the one I had fled in Ethiopia. The political system I had admired from far away appeared to be no different, with both major parties entrenched in their positions and increasingly unwilling to work together for the country's future.

The political polarization in America represents a deeper issue of identity, culture, and trust. Just as the communities I grew up in fell apart due to unresolved political conflict, I fear that America could face the same fate if this trajectory continues unchecked. The rise of partisan media and misinformation exacerbates these divides, reminiscent of the propaganda that fueled tensions in my homeland. When used as a weapon, political rhetoric fosters an "us versus them" mentality that tears at the social fabric.

This growing discontent is a haunting echo of my past, urging me to act. My experiences have instilled in me a deep conviction that we must not take our democratic processes for granted. The lessons I learned in Tigray still resonate within me, pushing me to advocate for change and uphold the values of unity and empathy. In an increasingly divided world, we must remember that we are all interconnected and that our collective well-being depends on understanding one another's tribulations.

## CHANGING OUTLOOKS ON IMMIGRATION

Over the past three decades, the global approach to immigration and refugee resettlement has changed significantly. Once, many countries actively sought to welcome immigrants through formal and regulated processes, understanding the mutual benefits of such resettlement. However, today, the political appetite for accepting immigrants has declined, driven by various known and unclear factors. Policies have become more restrictive, and the willingness to accept immigrants—especially refugees—has diminished noticeably.

Even for those seeking legal immigration pathways, the process has become increasingly challenging. Attempting to enter countries illegally is now more perilous and fraught with danger. I strongly advise taking such unsafe routes, as the risks to personal safety are immense. Instead, the focus should address the underlying causes that compel people to leave their homeland. Developing countries must work in partnership with foreign governments to improve economic conditions and governance, fostering environments where citizens can build prosperous lives without feeling the need to flee. Additionally, foreign aid should be contingent upon these improvements.

Donor countries should also reconsider how they provide foreign aid. Direct support to undemocratic governments often perpetuates corruption and undermines progress. Assistance should be dependent upon measurable improvements in human rights and good governance. By holding governments accountable, we can create the conditions necessary for long-term development and stability, reducing the need for people to seek refuge in other countries under dangerous and uncertain circumstances.

Reflecting on my journey from being a refugee to becoming a U.S. soldier, I've come to appreciate the profound need for leadership that not only protects democracy but also fosters unity. My experiences have shown me that America's strength lies in its diversity and the voices that come together to uphold the values of freedom and justice. As the nation moves forward, it must heed the lessons of history and reflect on the steep costs of polarization. The divisions threatening to tear the country apart, in the end, healing can only be through a steadfast commitment to open dialogue, collaboration across all boundaries, and a collective dedication to the common good.

As I contemplate the future of this country, one question lingers: will we be able to overcome the forces that seek to divide us? Just as I fought to establish my place in this nation, I believe the American people can unite to combat the ordeals facing our democracy, ensuring it serves all citizens, regardless of background or belief. Yet, the path ahead is uncertain, and the stakes have never been higher. The future hinges on whether we, as a people, can choose unity over division and embrace the rich diversity of voices and perspectives that truly make America strong.

The answer remains to be seen, but one thing is clear: the fight for unity and democracy is not over. It is a battle that will require resilience, courage, and the will to come together—just as I have throughout my journey. The pressing question is whether we, as a nation, possess the energy to rise to those obstacles.

When the tasks of hardship became overwhelming, my faith held me together. God's guidance reminded me that every setback was a step toward something more significant. In every prayer, I found peace, knowing that He was orchestrating my next move.

## NAVIGATING CONFLICT

Conflict is an inevitable part of life. Whether it arises from personal relationships, professional challenges, or broader societal issues, conflict tests our resilience, values, and problem-solving abilities. While it often feels uncomfortable or even overwhelming, conflict holds the potential for profound growth and transformation. The key to navigating conflict is not simply to avoid or resolve it but to understand the valuable lessons it offers.

One of the first lessons conflict teaches is *self-awareness*. In the heat of disagreement or struggle, emotions can run high, and it's easy to react impulsively. However, the ability to step back, pause, and assess the situation allows us to recognize how we respond—not just to the conflict itself but to the underlying emotions, fears, or insecurities that may influence our behavior. By cultivating self-awareness, we gain the clarity needed to approach the situation more calmly and thoughtfully, avoiding rash decisions that might escalate the conflict further.

Conflict also offers the opportunity to develop **empathy**. When we face disagreements, particularly with people we care about, it can be easy to focus solely on our

140

perspective. However, listening deeply to the other person's viewpoint can provide valuable insight into their feelings and needs. Empathy allows us to connect with others on a human level, even when we disagree. It helps us understand that conflict often arises from unmet needs or misunderstandings rather than malice or ill intentions. Through empathy, we can approach conflict not as an adversary but as a chance to foster mutual understanding and strengthen our relationships.

Another key lesson learned in times of struggle is *resilience*. Conflict often forces us to face adversity head-on, and how we respond can shape our personal growth. Rather than being defeated by difficult circumstances, we learn to adapt and persist, finding ways to bounce back from setbacks. Resilience is not just about enduring; it's about emerging stronger and wiser from the experience. Each challenge we face teaches us new skills, whether they are emotional coping mechanisms, communication strategies, or problem-solving approaches that we can apply in future situations.

Moreover, conflict provides the opportunity to clarify and *reinforce our values*. When faced with difficult decisions or moral dilemmas, our choices reveal what we truly stand for. Navigating conflict forces us to evaluate our priorities and determine what is most important to us, whether it's personal integrity, the well-being of others, or a commitment to fairness. In times of struggle, our values guide us through chaos, helping us make decisions aligned with our true selves and enabling us to act with purpose and conviction.

Communication is another essential lesson learned during conflict. Disputes often arise from a breakdown in communication, whether due to misinterpretation, lack of clarity, or emotional reactions that cloud understanding. By honing our communication skills, being clear, direct, and respectful, we can prevent conflicts from escalating and resolve misunderstandings more effectively. Sometimes, asking the right questions or actively listening can open the door to a resolution.

Finally, navigating conflict teaches us about *the importance of compromise*. Life rarely offers clear-cut solutions, especially when different interests, opinions, and values are involved. Conflict often requires us to find a middle ground, balancing our own needs with the needs of others. The willingness to compromise doesn't mean sacrificing our principles; instead, it involves finding creative solutions that honor both sides and foster collaboration. Compromise is essential for maintaining healthy relationships and building stronger, more resilient communities.

In the end, the lessons learned in times of conflict are invaluable. Conflict challenges us to grow emotionally, mentally, and spiritually, pushing us to become more empathetic, resilient, and self-aware. By embracing conflict as an opportunity for learning and growth, we transform struggles into bridges toward a more fulfilling, purposeful life. The ability to navigate conflict with grace and wisdom enhances our personal development. It deepens our connections with others, creating more potent, more compassionate communities.

## THE POWER OF UNWAVERING BELIEF

How do we stand firm against life's most significant internal and external tests? Sometimes, it feels like a relentless storm, tearing through everything you've built and leaving you on the brink of collapse. Yet, like a tree with deep, unyielding roots, you can endure even the fiercest tempests. Setbacks are inevitable; they are woven into the fabric of life itself.

To overcome them, you must awaken the force within—a force more potent than the pressure surrounding you. Through the teachings of Christ, I've discovered that no storm lasts forever. Each trial, no matter how painful, has been a lesson in courage, resilience, and growth.

The storms of life no longer hold power over me. They do not define who I am but have shaped me into someone more substantial and more purposeful. Every hardship has tested my character, refined it, and shown me that the benefit can emerge from even the darkest moments.

You, too, have this energy within you. Embrace it. Let every test you face be an opportunity to deepen your roots, knowing with certainty that the hardship will go, and you will emerge stronger, ready to achieve your most significant promise.

## Chapter 6: FRESH START IN THE SOUTH

The cultural differences between my birthplace in Ethiopia and the United States are profound. In Ethiopia, community living was tightly woven, with traditions, customs, and values passed down through generations. Family was the heart of everything; meals, celebrations, and even discussions on social issues were shared among extended relatives."

This version keeps the essence intact while providing a smoother flow and more emphasis on the centrality of family. Life moved at a slower, more deliberate pace, shaped by agricultural seasons and the rhythms of daily survival. A deep sense of responsibility toward others, especially family, was instilled in me, rooted in respecting elders and maintaining a collective sense of belonging. This environment taught me the importance of interdependence and cooperation, where every individual's contribution mattered for the well-being of the larger community.

In contrast, the United States introduced me to a stimulating but disorienting world. It operated on a fast-paced, individualistic mindset that placed personal independence above all else. Success was often measured by individual achievement rather than collective harmony. While the culture of self-reliance and ambition opened doors to opportunities I had never imagined, it also clashed with my genuinely ingrained sense of community. Navigating this cultural shift wasn't easy; it required adopting new norms and reevaluating my identity in a society where individualism governed supreme.

Adjusting to this environment meant embracing values that initially felt foreign. For example, I had to grow comfortable with the directness of American communication. In Ethiopia, we are taught to be more reserved, often using indirect language to show respect for other's feelings. In the U.S., people express their opinions and emotions freely. Although this openness was harsh at first, I later came to appreciate it, as it taught me the importance of clarity and assertiveness in relationships. Similarly, American traditions like Thanksgiving introduced me to new ways of celebrating community, offering moments of reflection and gratitude that echoed the communal values I had grown up with—although in a different form.

Nevertheless, the fast pace of life and the emphasis on time management posed some of the most significant

147

challenges. In Ethiopia, time was fluid—a concept based on relationships and shared moments. In America, time is a resource to maximize productivity and efficiency. This shift influenced my professional life and reshaped how I approached personal relationships and even my sense of purpose.

Despite these adjustments, I held tightly to many aspects of my heritage. The values of humility, respect for others, and the importance of family remained central to my identity. These principles guided how I interacted with the world and anchored me as I adapted to the demands of life in the United States. Balancing these values with the American ideals of freedom and self-expression allowed me to create a unique identity that honored the traditions of my past while embracing the opportunities of my present. Living between two worlds requires a delicate balance.

On one hand, I sought to preserve the values that had shaped me- communal responsibility, humility, and respect for tradition. On the other, I needed to adopt the individualism and ambition characteristic of American culture. This balancing act became a recurring theme in my personal and professional growth. It demanded constant negotiation between my roots and the opportunities afforded me by life in the U.S.

This negotiation extended to my relationships. In my culture, social fabrics and connections were built through shared time and mutual dependence. In the U.S., friendships and professional relationships often felt more like transactional. Succeeding in the American workplace required self-promotion and confidence—traits initially felt at odds with the humility taught. Over time, I realized that my values didn't conflict with American ideals but could enhance them. By integrating respect, community, and cooperation into the fast-paced world of American ambition, I developed a personal approach to success that felt authentic and sustainable.

## SETTLING IN FLORIDA

My internal negotiation reached a turning point when I decided to settle in Jacksonville, Florida. After years of service, education, and navigating the challenges of immigrant life, this moves symbolized more than a change of scenery—it represented a commitment to stability, community, and personal peace. Jacksonville marked the beginning of a new chapter, where I could fully embrace the blend of values that defined me.

Initially, Florida wasn't part of my long-term vision. After years of moving between refugee camps, military bases, and university campuses, I had imagined my future unfolding somewhere more familiar. But life, as it often does, had other plans. Florida's warm climate, diverse community, and proximity to nature quickly made it an appealing choice. With its blend of urban energy and coastal calm, Jacksonville offered a balance that felt right for this new phase of my life. It became a place to build a career, cultivate meaningful relationships, and embrace a slower, more intentional pace that allowed me to reflect on my journey and focus on the road ahead.

Arriving in Jacksonville was a mix of excitement and apprehension. I had experienced transitions before, but this one felt different. I wasn't just looking for a place to live. I was searching for a community to belong to. Florida's welcoming atmosphere and the warmth of its people eased the transition more than I expected. Jacksonville's neighborhoods, each with their unique charm, felt inviting. Before long, I found myself embraced by a diverse and supportive community. The city's mix of cultures mirrored my experiences, offering comfort and familiarity in this new chapter of my life.

One of my priorities after settling in Jacksonville was finding a spiritual anchor. My faith, an energy source throughout my life, guided me through uncertainty and connected me to my heritage. Discovering Debre Genet *Med han Alem*, Tigrayan Orthodox church, felt like finding a piece of home. The church became more than a place of worship—it was a sanctuary where I could reconnect with my cultural roots while embracing my new surroundings. Its prayers, rituals, and community gave me the grounding to approach this new chapter with clarity and purpose.

Jacksonville also became a place of professional growth. My computer science and cybersecurity background aligned well with the city's expanding tech sector. Attending local tech events and networking groups helped me connect with like-minded professionals who shared my passion for innovation. The city's tech community was collaborative and welcoming, providing the support I needed to build my career and develop my skills.

Yet my vision extended beyond personal success. I felt a profound responsibility to give back to the community that had welcomed me. Mentoring young people interested in technology became a side interest project. Having benefited from mentors throughout my journey, I understood the importance of guidance and encouragement. I began mentoring students in achieving a career, sharing my experiences, and providing them with the resources to pursue their dreams. These moments of connection gave my work a more profound sense of purpose.

My commitment to service wasn't limited to technology. As an immigrant, I felt a strong connection to initiatives supporting refugees. I knew the challenges they faced—the uncertainty, language barriers, and feelings of displacement—because I had lived through them myself. By partnering with advocacy groups, I shared my experiences and offered practical guidance to help others navigate their new lives. Whether assisting with paperwork or providing emotional support, I found immense fulfillment in helping newcomers adjust to their surroundings.

Mentorship also played a significant role in my work with veterans. I understood the difficulties of transitioning from that duty to civilian society. Military life's camaraderie, structure, and purpose often left a void when it ended. As a mentor, I aimed to provide practical advice and a sense of community. Helping veterans through social networks to navigate various issues and find new ways to connect, contribute, and thrive was deeply rewarding.

My dedication to mentorship extended to young people as well. Education had transformed my life, and I felt compelled to help the next generation recognize its power. Guiding students in their academic pursuits, guiding them to college entrance, or encouraging them to explore new paths brought me immense joy. These roles allowed me to see my journey in a new light—my success was not just about personal milestones but about the impact I could have on others.

The unexpected gift in Florida was the connection I found with nature. Jacksonville's fabulous beaches, river parks, and lush reserves provided a much-needed escape from the demands of daily life. After years in high-pressure environments—duty, academia, living in big cities like Washington D.C. and beyond—quiet moments outdoors became a refuge. Whether walking along the beach at sunrise, hiking nearby trails, or sitting by the river, I found time to reflect and recharge.

These moments in nature weren't just about relaxation but balance. Life's fast pace often left little room for introspection, but being outdoors allowed me to slow down and focus on what truly mattered. The grounding effect of nature reminded me of life's simple joys and provided clarity amidst obstacles.

## EMBRACING NEW BEGINNINGS

Although building a new life in Jacksonville wasn't smooth, those ordeals were controlled and transformed into touches. Like any major transition, it came with its fair share of doubt and difficulty. Adjusting to a new way of life, forging new friendships, and learning the quirks of unfamiliar problems tested my patience and resilience. I often missed the comfort of the life I had left behind and sometimes wondered if moving to Florida had been the right choice. But I reminded myself that every new chapter comes with its hurdles—and that growth often happens in the face of discomfort. The idea seems that comfort is the enemy of progress.

Over time, Jacksonville started to feel like home. The warmth of its people, the beauty of the surroundings, and the opportunities for personal and professional growth reassured me that I was exactly where I needed to be. I found peace knowing that this move honored my past and future. With gratitude and hope, I embraced this new chapter of my life.

## A LIFE SHAPED BY SERVICE

Reflecting on my journey to Jacksonville, I see it as more than just a physical, spiritual and emotional transformation. This chapter of my life has centered on balancing my heritage with my American identity, personal ambition with community responsibility, and the fast-paced demands of modern life with the quiet peace of nature. Jacksonville has offered me space to navigate these dualities and build a life rooted in personal fulfillment and service to others.

Creating a home in Florida has enriched my life in countless ways. It has allowed me to grow professionally, bond my connections to the community, and find support in the natural beauty surrounding me. More importantly, it has deepened my belief in the power of giving back. Whether through mentoring, advocacy, or simply being present for those who need support, I've understood that true joy lies in lifting others. It is the legacy I strive to build—a life defined by service, growth, and meaningful connection.

Still, as I reflect on this chapter, a lingering question remains: Can the peace and purpose I've found here withstand the inevitable hurdles ahead? My foundation—centered on service and community—feels firm. However, life's unpredictability has a way of testing even the most steadfast structures. The peace I've cultivated feels tangible, but will it hold firm when faced with the literal and metaphorical storms that are sure to come?

As I look to the future, I am reminded that growth is never static. There will always be new hurdles to face and new hurdles to overcome. But it is in confronting these uncertainties that I will continue to grow.

I continue to build upon this legacy, I strive to create a life that lifts and elevates those around me. The journey is far from over, and the path ahead remains uncertain. But with resilience and commitment to service, I know I am prepared for whatever lies beyond the horizon.

CONCLUSION: A TRANSFORMATIONAL
JOURNEY

Reflecting on the journey that took me from the remote
landscapes of Ethiopia to serving as a U.S. soldier, from
navigating the complexities of immigration to building a
successful career, profoundly touched by the lessons that
have shaped my life. This journey has been one of survival
and transformation, defined by hardship but, more
importantly, by resilience, faith, and an unwavering pursuit
of education and purpose.

My military service in the U.S. Army was pivotal to my
transformation. Over eight years of dedicated service,
having gained invaluable lessons honorably discharged that
profoundly deepened my understanding of serving. Serving
the nation is not just about fulfilling duties or following
orders; it is about honoring the commitment to sacrifice and
a collective responsibility to protect and support one
another. The discipline and camaraderie I found there
equipped me with qualities that continue to shape who I am
today. My service remains a testament to my gratitude
toward the nation that gave me the chance to rebuild my
life.

At the heart of my story lies an unshakable faith, which served as my compass during the most tumultuous times—whether fleeing conflict, adapting to new environments, or enduring the physical and emotional demands of military life. Faith anchored me when I felt crushed under responsibility and uncertainty. Even in moments of despair, my belief in a higher purpose gifted me the resilience to rise above adversity and pursue a meaningful life.

Education has been the great equalizer in my life. It gave me the tools to understand the world, seize opportunities, and shape my destiny. Each milestone—from earning my high school diploma to completing advanced degrees—represents academic achievement and triumph over obstacles that once seemed insurmountable. Education empowered me to move from survival to success in fields I once thought unreachable. This belief in the transformative power of knowledge remains the foundation of my mission to uplift others.

Yet, this journey extends beyond personal achievements. It is about giving back—paying forward the blessings and opportunities I have received. Whether mentoring young people, supporting fellow veterans, or helping immigrants navigate their paths, I have come to understand that my story intertwined with the lives of others. The support and guidance I received at critical moments, especially in foster care, inspired me to encourage and uplift those facing similar hurdles.

The families and individuals who opened their hearts and homes to me played pivotal roles in shaping my identity and resilience. Their kindness taught me that success is most meaningful when it uplifts others and helps build stronger, more compassionate communities. Success, I have learned, is not measured solely by personal accomplishments but by the impact we have on the lives of those around us.

Reflecting on the challenges and triumphs that have brought me to where I am today, I am grateful. My journey—from refugee to U.S. soldier, student to mentor, and uncertainty to purpose—proves the power of perseverance, faith, and the pursuit of knowledge. No challenge is impossible when faced with determination and a willingness to grow.

Looking to the future, I carry the lessons of my past and hope for what lies ahead. I remain committed to service, education, and living a life that reflects the values that have guided me thus far. My story is not just personal, it is shared with countless others who have faced hardship and found the strength to rebuild. It is a reminder of the extraordinary potential within each of us to transform our lives and, in doing so, make a lasting impact on the world around us.

This journey is about much more than survival. It is about thriving, finding purpose in every experience, and using that purpose to serve others. No matter where we begin, faith, education, and the support of a strong community can help us build futures defined by success, service, and lasting impact.

# APPENDICES

## VISUALIZE THE JOURNEY

This Google map traces my path, starting in January 1988 when, at the age of fourteen, I left my hometown of Idaga Hamous in Tigray, Ethiopia, in search of freedom. After crossing into Sudan, I encountered countless challenges that tested my resilience.

This version enhances emotional weight and clarity while keeping the focus on the journey and its hardships.

East Africa Map. Source (Google.com)

Leaving my home into Sudan, the long walk

From Tigray, the journey to freedom meant days of
walking to reach Sudan.

# READING RESOURCES

The following information was compiled from various online sources, organizations, and government websites to help readers explore support programs and resources:

- Veteran Support Organizations
  - *Department of Veterans Affairs (VA)*: Provides healthcare, education benefits, and disability compensation services. www.va.gov
  - *Disabled American Veterans (DAV)*: Assists disabled veterans in accessing benefits and employment opportunities. www.dav.org
- Educational Programs and Federal Student Aid
  - *Free Application for Federal Student Aid (FAFSA)*: Offers financial aid for college. www.studentaid.gov
  - *Microsoft Software and Systems Academy (MSSA)*: Free training for veterans transitioning to tech careers. www.microsoft.com
  - *Coursera*: Provides free and paid online courses from top institutions. www.coursera.org

- o *Upward Bound*: Federal program providing college prep for students from low-income families. www2.ed.gov/programs/trioupbound
- Post-9/11 GI Bill
  - o Administered by the VA to provide tuition assistance, housing stipends, and book funds for veterans. www.benefits.va.gov/gibill
- Refugee Support Organizations
  - o *International Rescue Committee (IRC)*: Offers education, employment, and emergency support for refugees worldwide. www.rescue.org
  - o *UNHCR (United Nations High Commissioner for Refugees)*: Protects and supports refugees with shelter, food, and resettlement services. www.unhcr.org
  - o *Ethiopian Community Development Council (ECDC)*: Assists refugees and marginalized communities in the U.S. www.ecdcus.org

State-Specific Resources
- New York:
  - o *NYC Mayor's Office of Immigrant Affairs*: Offers resources for immigrants and refugees, including educational programs. www.nyc.gov/immigrants

- California:
  - *California Department of Social Services – Refugee Programs*: Provides various refugee services and programs, including education. www.cdss.ca.gov/refugee-services
- Texas:
  - Offers various refugee services, including educational and vocational training. Check with local refugee service providers.
- Illinois:
  - *Illinois Refugee and Immigrant Services*: Provides educational resources and refugee support. www.dhs.state.il.us

## ABOUT THE AUTHOR

Berhane Amene is a veteran, cybersecurity consultant, and author whose life embodies resilience, faith, and the pursuit of success. Born in a small city and later forced to flee conflict, he grew up as a refugee before navigating life in foster care and ultimately joining the U.S. military.

Berhane's military service and academic achievements, including a master's degree in Cybersecurity Engineering, reflect his dedication to overcoming adversity and building a better future.

Today, Berhane resides in Florida, where he runs a cybersecurity consulting business and is actively involved in his community. Through his book, From Refugee to U.S. Soldier: A Journey of Faith and Success, he shares his story to inspire others to embrace faith, perseverance, and the courage to overcome the core tasks.

## CONNECT WITH THE AUTHOR

Thank you for reading my story! I'd love to stay connected with you. Explore more, follow me, or reach out using the links below:

### Websites

*Couragefy: www.couragefy.com*
*AM Cybersecurity: www.amcybersecurity.com*

### Email

*amcyber21@gmail.com*

### Social Media

*LinkedIn: linkedin.com/in/berhaneamene*
*Facebook: facebook.com/berhaneamene*
*Instagram: instagram.com/thundero20*

## ACKNOWLEDGMENTS

I want to express my sincere gratitude to all those who supported and guided me throughout this struggle. To my mentors and advisors, your insights and encouragement were invaluable in shaping this work. I am also deeply grateful to my colleagues and peers for their constructive feedback and thoughtful discussions.

Special thanks to those who provided emotional and practical support during challenging times. Your unwavering belief in me kept me going. Finally, to my loved ones, your constant presence and encouragement have bonded me. This work results from many contributions, and I am truly thankful to all of you.

THE END

www.ingramcontent.com/pod-product-compliance
Lightning Source LLC
Chambersburg PA
CBHW071747120626
46550CB00002B/695